M000216230

Who is Israel?

Redeemed Israel-
A Primer

Batya Ruth Wootten

Foreword by Angus Wootten

Who is Israel?
Redeemed Israel- *A Primer*
Batya Ruth Wootten Foreword by Angus Wootten

© 2011, Batya Ruth Wootten, Saint Cloud, FL, 34770
"Two Sticks" artwork by Crystal Lenhart. Cover design by John Diffenderfer, Tony Scheibelhut, and Batya Wootten.

All rights reserved under International and Pan-American Copyright Conventions. This book or parts thereof may not be reproduced in any form, stored in a retrieval system, or transmitted in any form by any means, electronic, mechanical, photocopy, recording, or otherwise, without prior written permission from the publisher. Brief quotations with credits may be used in critical reviews or articles.

Published and Distributed by:
Key of David Publishing, PO Box 700217, Saint Cloud, FL, 34770
www.keyofdavidpublishing.com
Also Distributed by:
Messianic Israel Marketplace, PO Box 3263, Lebanon, TN 37088
(800.829.8777) www.messianicisrael.com
Printed in the United States of America.

All quotations used by permission.

Unless otherwise noted, Scripture quotations are from the *New American Standard Bible®*, Copyright © 1960-1995, Lockman Foundation. All rights reserved. Used by permission, www.Lockman.org; and from Quick Verse for Windows, Electronic Edition STEP Files Copyright © 2003, QuickVerse, a division of Findex.com, Inc., all rights reserved.

Verses marked KJV are from the *King James Version* Bible.

Notes, Abbreviations, and Bibliography:

To emphasize some Scriptures, italics or an alternate word choice has been used, especially for the names of the Father and Son. Also, brackets [] indicate text added by the author.

The following abbreviations are used for reference purposes:

BDBL: *New Brown-Driver-Briggs-Gesenius Hebrew- Aramaic Lexicon*
NIV: *New International Version Study Bible*
Strong's: *Strong's Exhaustive Concordance*
S&BDB: *Strong's and Brown-Driver-Briggs together*
TWOT: *Theological Wordbook of the Old Testament*
Bibliography: Please see *Redeemed Israel— Reunited and Restored.*

Acknowledgments:

Thanks to the following friends for their invaluable counsel and editorial help: Sandy Bloomfield, Richard A. Erb, Jr., PC, Kate Maul, Dennis Northington, David Pennington, Dr. Georgina Perdomo, Eugene Porter, Rob Roy, Larry Schmidt, and Scott Skaggs.

ISBN 978-1886987-39-5

Word Definitions:

YHVH- יהוה

In this work we will occasionally use these four letters to indicate the Name of the One True God, which Name is often translated as "the LORD." Historically, Judaism avoided its use and Christianity followed suit. The Father's Name is spelled with four Hebrew letters, יהוה, yod, hey, vav, hey, and is variously translated: Yahweh, Yahveh, Yehovah, etc. We sometimes use the four English letters that best duplicate the sound of the Hebrew letters, as pronounced in modern Hebrew: YHVH. We also sometimes use *Elohim*, which is Hebrew for *God*, and Yah, which is short for YHVH (Isaiah 12:2).

Yeshua- ישוע

Yeshua is the Messiah's Hebrew/Aramaic name. A shortened form of Yehoshua (Joshua), it means "Salvation" (Nehemiah 8:17; Matthew 1:21). Jesus is derived from the Greek *Iesous*. The Greeks changed His name because their language did not have a "sh" sound, plus they often added an "s" to the end of male names. This Greek transliteration was converted into English at a time when the English letter "J" had a sound like that of today's "Y." It was pronounced "Yesus," much like the Greek name. But, with the hardening of the sound of the English "J," it began to be pronounced as "Jesus." We choose to transliterate His name from Hebrew into English as "Yeshua."

Ephraim- אפרים

Ephraim is the given name of Joseph's second son. It means *doubly fruitful*. Jacob/Israel prophesied that Ephraim's heirs would one day become a "fullness of Gentiles."

The name "Ephraim" is used in the scriptures to describe the ten tribes of the Northern Kingdom, which is also called the Kingdom of Israel. The term "Ephraimite" is sometimes used to describe these people (as opposed to the Southern Kingdom of Judah). The people of Ephraim lost their identity after they were exiled by the Assyrians (around 722 B.C.). We use this name to describe those known as the "ten lost tribes," and to *broadly* speak of non-Jewish Believers in the Messiah of Israel, who also are declared in Scripture to be full members of Messiah Yeshua's Commonwealth of Israel (Genesis 41:52; 1 Kings 12:21; 2 Kings 17:34; Ezekiel 37:15 -28; Ephesians 2:11-22).

Torah- תורה

Torah means teaching, instruction, direction. This Hebrew word is often translated as the "Law." Our God says He loved Abraham because he kept His Laws (Genesis 26:5). Abraham kept the spirit of the Torah before the letter of it was given to Moses. Everyone who wants to be blessed in life should look to our Father's precepts for guidance. Moses said of them, "Keep and do them, for that is your wisdom and your understanding in the sight of the peoples who will hear all these statutes and say, 'Surely this great nation is a wise and understanding people'" (Deuteronomy 4:5-6). King David said, "How blessed are those whose way is blameless, who walk in the Torah of the LORD. How blessed are those who observe His testimonies, who seek Him with all their heart. They also do no unrighteousness; they walk in His ways.... Oh that my ways may be established to keep Thy statutes! Then I shall not be ashamed" (Psalm 119:1-6).

King David also said of the Father's Word, "The sum of Your word is truth, and every one of Your righteous ordinances is everlasting" (Psalm 119:160). Messiah Yeshua, in a prayer for those who would follow Him, said of the written

Word of His day, "Sanctify them in the truth; Your word is truth" (John 17:17).

As New Covenant Believers we are saved by grace through faith and not by works, by the shed blood of our Messiah and by the word of our testimony (Revelation 12:11). It is with this understanding of all that our Messiah has done for us, and of the wise and simple faith of our forefather Abraham, that we speak of honoring the eternal wisdom of Torah and walking in its lifestyle.

We further note that Adam and Eve were sent outside the Garden for their sin, and that Israel was scattered among the nations for theirs. Not until Messiah returns us to His Promised Land and sprinkles us with "clean water" will we be fully empowered to walk in His eternal Torah. Until then, we nonetheless seek to have the Messiah's eternal truths written on our hearts, by His Holy Spirit. In this way we will be empowered to walk in His way, even as was promised to those who partake of the New Covenant (Jeremiah 31:31-33; Ezekiel 36:23-28; 37:15-28).

Abba- אבא

Aramaic for "Father." The *Targums* translate Hebrew into Aramaic and use 'abba' for "father" or "my father." *Ab* is *Father, ha'Ab* is *the Father*. The word alludes to the deep spiritual relationship between Believers and God the Father. [a]

Believer(s)

We choose to use the word *Believer(s)* to describe those who seek to follow Israel's Messiah and to walk as He walked. We trust that, in the end, He alone will decide who did or did not "believe:" in Him (Matthew 7:23; Act 16:1; 1 Corinthians 6:15,20; Galatians 3:9; 1 Peter 1:17-19).

---

[a] According to an *Old Testament Word Studies* article, Abba does not mean "Daddy" as is commonly taught. See http://www.christianleadershipcenter.org

O house
of Ephraim Israel
and house of Judah...
the Father called your name,
a green olive tree, beautiful in fruit
and form. But because of your sins, He
pronounced evil against you. Yet take heart,
O house of Israel, take heart O house of Judah,
for YHVH has promised: It will come about that after
I have uprooted and scattered them, after some have
become like degenerate, foreign vines, then My compassions will again be kindled and I will regather them.
I will bring them back, each one to his own inheritance,
each one to his own land. Yes, this is My promise to
them. For these two olive branches are My two
chosen witnesses. And I will grant authority to
them, for they are the two sons of fresh oil
who are standing by the LORD
of all the earth.
(Jeremiah
2:18-21;
11:10,16
-17; 12:15;
Hosea 1-2;
Zechariah 4:11-14;
Revelation 11:3-4.)

Israel's Prophetic Call

"O House of Israel and House of Judah... YHVH called your name, 'A green olive tree, beautiful in fruit and form'" (Jeremiah 11:10,16). And YHVH says, "Behold, I will take the stick of Joseph, which is in the hand of Ephraim, and the tribes of Israel, his companions; and I will put them with the stick of Judah, and make them one stick... in My hand" (Ezekiel 37:19). "In those days the house of Judah will walk with the house of Israel, and they will come together... to the land I gave their fathers as an inheritance" (Jeremiah 3:18). "It will come about that just as you were a curse among the nations, O house of Judah and house of Israel, so I will save you that you may become a blessing. Do not fear; let your hands be strong" (Zechariah 8:13). "Then the jealousy of Ephraim will depart, and those who harass Judah will be cut off; Ephraim will not be jealous of Judah, and Judah will not harass Ephraim. They will swoop down on the slopes of the Philistines on the west; and YHVH will utterly destroy the tongue of the Sea of Egypt; and He will wave His hand over the River with His scorching wind; and He will strike it into seven streams and make men walk over dry-shod" (Isaiah 11:13-15). "'In those days and at that time,' declares YHVH, 'the sons of Israel will come, both they and the sons of Judah as well; they will go along weeping as they go, and it will be YHVH their God that they will seek. They will ask for the way to Zion, turning their faces in its direction; they will come that they may join themselves to YHVH in an everlasting covenant that will not be forgotten'" (Jeremiah 50:4-5).

"'Behold, days are coming,' declares YHVH, 'when I will make a new covenant with the house of Israel and with the house of Judah, not like the covenant which I made with their fathers in the day I took them by the hand to bring them out of the land of Egypt, My covenant which they broke, although I was a husband to them... But this is the covenant which I will make with the house of Israel after those days... I will put My law within them and on their heart I will write it; and I will be their God, and they shall be My people. They will not teach again, each man his neighbor and each man his brother, saying, "Know YHVH," for they will all know Me, from the least of them to the greatest of them... for I will forgive their iniquity, and their sin I will remember no more" (Jeremiah 31:31-34). "Therefore through this Jacob's iniquity will be forgiven; and this will be the full price of the pardoning of his sin: when he makes all the altar stones like pulverized chalk stones; when Asherim and incense altars will not stand" (Isaiah 27:9). "Return to the stronghold, O prisoners who have the hope; this very day I am declaring that I will restore double to you. For I will bend Judah as My bow, I will fill the bow with Ephraim... and I will make you like a warrior's sword. Then YHVH will appear over them, and His arrow will go forth like lightning; and the Lord YHVH will blow the trumpet, and will march in the storm winds of the south" (Zechariah 9:12-14).

Shema Israel,
Hear O Israel,
Hear and obey the call of the Holy One of Israel.

THERE ARE TWO MAIN BRANCHES IN THE OLIVE TREE OF ISRAEL:

EPHRAIM AND JUDAH

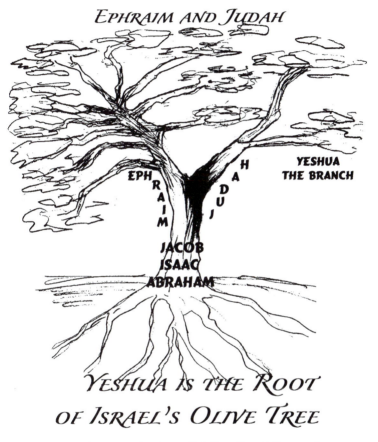

YESHUA IS THE ROOT OF ISRAEL'S OLIVE TREE

When the Father first called "Israel" an "olive tree,"
He specifically said He was speaking to
"the house of Israel and the house of Judah" (Jer 11:10).
Yeshua said, "I am the root and the offspring of David."
Isaiah calls the Messiah "the Branch"
(Rev 22:16; Isa 11:1).
(See pages 58-62 for more information.)

The Five Stages of Israel's Olive Tree

Jeremiah's Olive Tree
With Both Branches:
Ephraim and Judah
(Jer 11:10,16)

1

2

Ephraim's Branches
First to be Broken Off
Dispersed Among the
Nations (722 B.C.)
(Hos 1-2; 8:8; Amos 9:9)

3

4

Judah's Broken
Branches Dispersed to
Babylon (586 B.C.)
(Psa 137; 2 Ki 20:17; 24:15)

Paul's Olive Tree: 30 A.D.
With Some From
Judah Who Returned
From Babylon (Rom 11)

Israel's Restored
Olive Tree With
"Both Branches"
(*etz/sticks/branches/trees*).
Made One Stick/Tree
in the Father's Hand
(Eze 37:15-28)
(See pages 58-62
for more information)

Contents

Our Israelite Roots

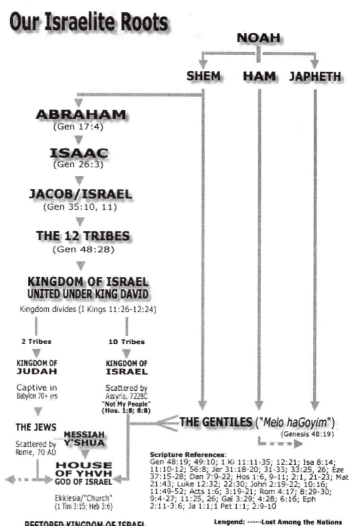

NOAH

SHEM **HAM** **JAPHETH**

ABRAHAM
(Gen 17:4)

ISAAC
(Gen 26:3)

JACOB/ISRAEL
(Gen 35:10, 11)

THE 12 TRIBES
(Gen 48:28)

KINGDOM OF ISRAEL
UNITED UNDER KING DAVID

Kingdom divides (I Kings 11:26-12:24)

2 Tribes

10 Tribes

KINGDOM OF
JUDAH

KINGDOM OF
ISRAEL

Captive in
Babylon 70+ yrs

Scattered by
Assyria, 722BC
"Not My People"
(Hos. 1:8; 8:8)

THE GENTILES ("*Melo haGoyim*")
(Genesis 48:19)

THE JEWS

MESSIAH
Y'SHUA

Scattered by
Rome, 70 AD

HOUSE
OF YHVH
GOD OF ISRAEL

Ekklesia/"Church"
(1 Tim 3:15; Heb 3:6)

Scripture References:
Gen 48:19; 49:10; 1 Ki 11:11-35; 12:21; Isa 8:14;
11:10-12; 56:8; Jer 31:18-20; 31-33; 33:25, 26; Eze
37:15-28; Dan 7:9-22; Hos 1:6, 9-11; 2:1, 21-23; Mat
21:43; Luke 12:32; 22:30; John 2:19-22; 10:16;
11:49-52; Acts 1:6; 3:19-21; Rom 4:17; 8:29-30;
9:4-27; 11:25, 26; Gal 3:29; 4:28; 6:16; Eph
2:11-3:6; Ja 1:1; 1 Pet 1:1; 2:9-10

Lengend: ------Lost Among the Nations

RESTORED KINGDOM OF ISRAEL
UNITED UNDER THE SON OF DAVID, MESSIAH Y'SHUA

Foreword

It is my observation that the God of Israel often uses men and women working together to keep His plan for Israel on course. Sometimes He especially chooses to use the female team member. For example, He used Sarah to ensure that the promise went to Isaac rather than to Ishmael (the one Abraham planned to choose), and He used Rebekah to thwart Isaac's plan to pass the promise to Esau rather than to Jacob (whom YHVH had chosen) (Genesis 21:9-12; 27:4-10).

I am thankful that the Father has used my wife, Batya, and her faithfulness to help keep our team on course. Because of her tenacity, we can now understand "Israel," and can therefore be used by the Holy One to help accomplish His desire, which is to have a people for His own possession.

In the early seventies we became deeply involved in what was then a new Messianic Jewish Movement, where we faced two initial challenges. First, we needed to provide a way for Jewish Believers to come to know Jesus, or Yeshua, as their Messiah without having to renounce their Jewish heritage. Secondly, we needed to present Israel's Messiah to the Church from a Jewish perspective, and thus encourage an appreciation for the eternal principles of Torah (the "Law") and for the truths revealed in the Feasts of Israel.

From the beginning, the movement began to attract so-called "Gentiles." In fact, more non-Jews were flocking to the Hebraic standards being raised by Messianic Judaism than were Jewish people. These Believers had two primary motivations: They wanted to support their Jewish brethren and they wanted to trade in their errant traditions for the Father's Torah truths and His eternal Feasts. They too were being drawn to this reemerging Israel.

We strongly supported the fledgling efforts of our Jewish brothers. Among other things, we established a real first: The *House of David Messianic Materials Catalogue*.

The goal of this publication was to develop and distribute materials that would aid Believers in understanding both their "roots" and the Jewish people.

However, the more we read and observed, the more we became concerned over the place being given to those who were regarded as non-Jews. At the time, Messianic Jewish heritage was based on the person having "visible" Jewish parentage when they became involved in the movement (or they could be married to someone who met their requirement). The "physical Jews" who accepted Messiah were assumed to be "spiritual Jews" as well. On the other hand, the "Gentiles" who joined the movement were considered to be only "spiritual" heirs, and there was no way for them to attain the Jewish "twice chosen" status.

This standard resulted in two classes of citizenship— a division that soon began to cause problems—because many non-Jews felt like they were being treated like second-class citizens.

Seeking resolution, I appealed to the leadership to establish a "conversion procedure" that would make everyone equal, both "physically" and "spiritually." However, not only was this proposal unacceptable to most of them, but after contemplating the idea, it became completely unacceptable to my wife. She reasoned that, while all must repent, if one also had to "be converted to be a first-class citizen," then one must have been born wrong in the first place. She would often say, *"A mortal man's declaration will not change the facts of who I am. What I need to know is, who am I to the Father?"*

The teachings being put forth about the roles of Israel and the Church did not seem to add up to what we saw in Holy Writ. This fact, plus the challenge of finding Scriptural books about Israel for our catalogue, led Batya to cry out to the Father for an answer to what had become for her, an ever-present question: *"Who is Israel?"*

This concise book offers the essence of the Father's answer to that important question. Surely the Holy Spirit will use this little book even as he has used its parent books to forever change multiplied thousands of lives.

Batya has written a number of books on this subject, with each new issue being more concise yet offering more material. Her best known book began a series titled, *Who Is Israel?* Her latest and best book is *Redeemed Israel—Reunited and Restored*. This work is an overview of many of her life-changing books.

Our prayer is that this economical "Primer" version will be used to help guide a believing Israel back onto the road of "Thy Kingdom come on earth, as it is in heaven." We pray that it will be used to help get the whole house of Israel back on course, thus preparing the way for Messiah's return and restoration of the Kingdom to Israel.

This brief work provides essential answers to the "Israel" question. It shows that Israel was divided into two houses (the house of Ephraim/Israel and the house of Judah.) It emphasizes the fact that our Father is now putting these brothers (and their companions) back together. And it touches on other life-changing questions, like, *Where is Israel now and what is her destiny?*

On a profoundly personal level, this solution-driven book will help you answer the following questions: *Who are you to the Father? Why do you feel the way you do about Israel? And, what is your individual destiny?*

I believe my wife was called to write the first of our books because in our team she is the "nit-picker" (you need one of those for research purposes). She is never willing to settle for anything less than the absolute truth, regardless of the consequences. Furthermore, between the two of us, she is more articulate. But her books speak for both of us. Every word. However, I feel there is another reason that she especially has been called to write on this subject. I think YHVH probably wanted this latter-day truth to be presented first by the feminine side of His creation, because in order to reunite a divided Israel, we need to see that Ephraim/Israel and Judah, Christians and Jews, often behave like battling, jealous children. And, before their age-old disputes can truly be settled, both must be corrected fairly and equitably (Deuteronomy 25:13-16; Proverbs 20:10). In the Father's grand design, mothers most often settle squabbles between children. Moreover, as reunited Israel comes forth from their womb of dispersion, they will be like sons who must first learn to heed their "mother's *instructions*" (Proverbs 1:8; 6:20). Scripture commands us not to "forsake the *law/torah* of our mother." And, our Mother's "torah," her particular female type of instruction, most often deals with the child's *heart attitude.*[b]

A child's training primarily begins with its mother. Only when a son has matured and developed a right heart attitude is he turned over to his father, who then teaches him the wisdom and eternal truths of Torah—he trains him to become *"bar mitzvah"* (a son of the commandments).

---

b For more information on this subject, see the book, *Mama's Torah: The Role of Women* by Batya Wootten, 2004, 2010, Key of David Publishing, Saint Cloud, FL. This book is receiving rave reviews from men and women alike.

This natural order teaches us that a right heart attitude is essential in order to be properly trained in the Father's Torah. Since women are usually more intuitive than men, they are generally much better at reaching the heart of a matter than are fact-oriented man. To put Israel back together again, we need to first become like little children and first deal with the issues of our hearts.

It also seems to me that our Father has often used women to get the men moving, and this generation of men needs to have a fire of faithfulness lit under them. There are too many who would rather sit and look for signs than move out and create wonders.

In the spirit of Deborah of old, Batya issues a call to those who are sitting and waiting like Barak. Hers is an encouraging call to *"Arise, O sons of Israel! Believe that the Father has given your enemies into your hands!"* (Judges 4-5). Her call is a declaration, for the exciting day is now upon us when the Holy One of Israel is beginning to make the "sticks" of Ephraim and Judah one stick in His holy hand (Ezekiel 37:15-28)!

This book is a collection of brief studies about both of the houses of Israel, and about their role in this exciting event. Each chapter adds new understanding to the whole. In the end, I think you will find the information contained herein will lead to a paradigm shift in your thinking. You will have a new and exciting Scriptural view of the whole house of Israel.

Today is the day when YHVH *Tsavaot*, the LORD of Hosts, is calling forth the overcoming armies of Israel! So sign up with Him today! Enlist right now! You do not want to miss out on all of the upcoming action!

He has sovereignly decreed that Ephraim and Judah ultimately will know victory over their enemies. They will help prepare the way for the return of our King and will help establish His kingdom here on earth (Isaiah 11:11-16).

We want to be part of that overcoming army. We want to partake of that victory.

Finally, I want to say that the God-given insight found in our books has brought radical change to my life. The scriptural insights offered have truly helped to remold me, to make me more aware of my ultimate destiny in Messiah, and to encourage me to walk in that destiny.

Furthermore, I have seen this same understanding dramatically change the lives of multiplied tens of thousands, and I know it can change you! So let me welcome you to the ranks of the radically changed. Let me welcome you to the multitude of forerunners who are now being prepared for the day when the kingdoms of this world will become the restored Kingdom of Israel!

Angus Wootten
Director
Key of David Publishing
Saint Cloud, Florida

One

Who is Israel?
And Why You Need to Know

Who is Israel?
Why do we even need to know? Is it not enough for Believers to know that we are "in Messiah"?

Our answers to these questions are extremely important. They set the course for how we interpret Scripture, how we determine who the Father's "chosen" people are, and how we define His end-time plan for them.

Whether realized or not, our answers to these questions play a profound role in our lives. In the game plan of the God of Israel, the people of Israel are the primary players. If we do not know who His players are, we will not understand His game plan or be able to properly play the game.

The people of Israel are the family of the God of Israel. They are His chosen people. But who makes up this family, the Jewish people or the New Covenant Believers?

For ages, the answers given by many Christians excluded those in Judaism. However, in our day, some give answers that similarly exclude New Covenant Believers from being part of the chosen people of Israel. Such denials have reaped an abundance of negative results for both groups. Both attitudes are unscriptural and only add to the problem.

To solve the Israel dilemma some teach that the Jewish people are "God's Chosen People" and that the Church is the "Bride of Christ." But Jesus Christ (Messiah Yeshua) said He is One with the Father. It was over this very claim that the Jews took up rocks to stone Him (John 10:30-31).

In truth, our Messiah is One with Him who says He chose Israel for His own possession, and that, only if the heavens above can be measured will He cast off all the offspring of Israel. He also vows that, "If I have not established my covenant with day and night and the fixed laws of heaven and earth, then I will reject the descendants of Jacob" (Deuteronomy 7:6; Jeremiah 31:37; 33:25-26).[1]

The immeasurable Heavens remain. Israel's offspring continue to be the chosen people of the God of Israel. He continues to love the people of Judah and has sworn that He "will possess Judah as His portion in the holy land and again choose Jerusalem" (Zechariah 2:12).

And yet...

In the New Covenant Peter writes to certain "aliens" (foreigners/strangers) and says, "You are *a chosen race*, a royal priesthood, a holy nation, a people for God's own possession" (1 Peter 1:1; 2:9). Paul likewise writes to non-Jewish Believers and tells them, "God has *chosen you* from the beginning for salvation" (2 Thessalonians 2:13).

So what is the truth? Who are the chosen people? Is it the Jewish people or the aliens to whom Peter wrote?

Answers found in Scripture will help us to better grasp God's end-time plan to re-gather His chosen people. They will also answer a question many non-Jewish Believers ask about themselves: *Who am I to the God of Israel?*

To begin, we note that YHVH says, "Israel is My son, My firstborn" (Exodus 4:22). If we reverse this statement we see that His "firstborn is Israel. "

---

1 Also see John 17:22; 1 Cor 8:6; 1 Tim 2:5; Deu 6:4; 7:6; 14:2; Mk 12:29; Exo 5:1-2; 2 Sam 7:24; Jer 30:1; 33:22,24; 46:28; Rom 11:2-5,26-29.

Who is Israel? And Why You Need to Know

To be Israel is to be the Father's firstborn. Messiah is the firstborn of all creation and the firstborn from the dead. In Him, we are called to the general assembly and *ekklesia,* or congregation, of the firstborn. In the spirit of Messianic prophecy YHVH says, "I am a father to Israel and Ephraim[2] [Joseph's firstborn heir] is My firstborn" (Jeremiah 31:9; Romans 8:29; Colossians 1:15,18; Hebrews 1:6; 12:23-24).

To be firstborn Israel is to have both a position and a call. Yet, many are content to apply this title to themselves in an abstract, spiritual sense. Others feel it makes no difference whether or not they are part of the people of Israel. *"We're the Church,"* they proudly assert. Or, they say, *"Why should we care about being part of Israel?"*

We care because the Holy One of Israel never made a covenant with Gentiles. He instead made His promised New Covenant with the House of Israel. And, in Messiah, we are called to join that covenant people and to be part of His holy commonwealth (Jeremiah 31:31-33; Hebrews 8:8-12; Ephesians 2:11-22). In short, we are either part of His designated covenant people—or we have no covenant at all.

We also care about who Israel is because we do not want to follow in Esau's foolish footsteps. The New Covenant sternly warns, "See that no one is…godless like Esau, who …sold his inheritance rights as the oldest son." Then, when he later wanted to inherit that blessing, he was rejected and could bring about no change of mind, though he sought for it with tears (Hebrews 12:15-17, NIV).

Esau could never regain what he had lost. In regard to inheritance, he was the actual firstborn son of Isaac, but he sold his birthright to his younger brother, Jacob for a bowl of beans. Thus did Esau despise his birthright, and he has been hated for his action ever since.[3]

---

2 Please see "Ephraim" in the Definitions Section (pages iii-iv).
3 Gen 25:22-34; 31:15; 37:28,36; Psa 73:18; 74:3; Rom 9:13; Heb 12:16; Mal 1:2-4; Obad 1:6-9,17-18; Jer 49:10.

This is not an Old Covenant story that we can summarily dismiss. These stories were recorded for *our* instruction. Again, we are called to Mount Zion, to the general assembly and *ekklesia* of the firstborn, to Messiah Yeshua, the mediator of a new covenant. And we are sternly warned not to think lightly of His high and holy call. We must instead regard it with proper reverence and awe (1 Corinthians 10:1,11; Hebrews 12:18-28).

Esau was called a "profane" man because he gave away that which should have been precious to him. Similarly, for us to think lightly of our call to belong to the *ekklesia* of Firstborn Israel is to risk a sin like that of Esau. We do not want to be like him, or even be one of his neighbors, for they too were destroyed (Romans 9:13; Jeremiah 49:10).

To have our Father call us His firstborn is to be given a priceless gift. Like Jacob, with unflinching determination, we must hold on until we receive our blessing. Jacob endured wrestling with the angel and would not quit, and thus was given the title of "Israel"—meaning *he who prevails* (Genesis 32:26-30).

In Israel, the firstborn would inherit a double portion and a certain right to rule. In turn, he would be the next head of his family.[4] His call was to be like a redeemer to his brethren when they were in a time of need. This is a role that is of profound importance, especially in the times in which we now live...

Again we ask, who are the Father's "chosen" people?

Is it the Christians or the Jews? Or, could the Scriptural answer include both groups of people? Moreover, could it be that we have not understood this Scriptural truth because we were not meant to fully understand about "all Israel" until this point in time in history?[5]

We suggest that this is the case.

---

4 Deu 21:17; *Strong's Concordance* #'s H 4941 and 1062.
5 Ref Deu 7:6; 1 Pet 1:1; 2:9; Isa 8:13-14; Rom 11:25.

To properly answer our questions about Israel we must address the idea of "Physical Israel." We cannot conclude this matter unless we do so, but we do so with a caveat. We will not examine Israel's blessings in an attempt to prove patriarchal descent for any person or group. We instead do so for the following reasons:

Most people define Israel based on some idea of physical descent, regardless of how abstract or vague their definition. Perceived physical descent from the patriarchs, or a presumed lack thereof, is most often the deciding factor in everyone's "Israel decision." Therefore, if we want to understand Israel, we are *forced* to address this universal standard because it is the underlying and misleading presumption in most conclusions in the matter. We challenge the validity of this misconceived rule, because the errant answers that have grown out of it have affected the very fundamentals of our faith. For, when coming to know Messiah Yeshua, one naturally asks the questions, "Who are His chosen people? Who are Abraham's heirs? Who is Israel?"

To understand the foundational truths of our faith, we must have Scriptural answers to these questions. We also examine this issue because the results of denying the Jewish people their rightful position as part of the people of Israel is a sin of monumental proportions—and it must be stopped. However, to similarly deny the non-Jew his rightful position as part of the people of Israel is also a sin of profound proportions, and must also be stopped.

Our study will be rooted in the beliefs that people cannot absolutely prove genetic connection to the patriarchs, for reasons like rape and adultery, plus, destruction of the Temple in 70 A.D. resulted in all official lineage documents being destroyed. For these and other reasons, we do not suggest anyone actually pursue "endless genealogies" (1 Timothy 1:4). We conclude that it is pointless for anyone to be argumentative about this issue, or try to make arrogant claims based on unprovable genealogy.

This means that Jewish people cannot prove they are physically related to Abraham and no one can prove that non-Jewish Believers are not physically descended from him. Lineage simply cannot be proven either way.

Because no one can absolutely prove that they descend from the patriarchs, we pursue our course by faith alone, using Scripture as our guidebook. We press on in hopes that we might restore to a people of promise that which was once lost.[6] We do so in hopes that Messiah's followers will be inspired with a great sense of latter-day destiny.

Finally, we must understand that even though people sometimes offer complicated theories about Israel, the truth about her identity is really very simple to understand:

Long ago the Father divided Israel into two houses, Ephraim (Israel) and Judah. As His "two witnesses," He sent them in two different directions to serve two principal purposes—to establish His two immutable truths of Law and Salvation by Grace. And now, in this last day, YHVH would have His two Israels come together, that they might fulfill His divine purpose and begin to more fully confirm His truth in the earth.[7]

That is the simple truth behind this book.

As you read the confirming verses in this condensed overview, please remember the simplicity behind it all:

Two houses—Two directions—Two different purposes —Now is the time to put them back together again.

Father, we seek Your truth concerning Israel. We want to be led by Your Holy Spirit and kept from all error. We ask that, as we study, we might hear Your voice alone as You quietly whisper in our ear, "This is the way, walk ye in it" (Isaiah 30:21).

Amen and Amen.

---

6 Deu 30:3; Isa 11:1-14; 49:6; Jer 31:21; 33:7; Hos 1-2; Acts 15:16.
7 Ref: 1 Ki 11:11-12,26,31-35; 12:24; Isa 43:10;

Two

Many Israels-One Israel

To understand Israel we will first look to the most important Israel of all. Basically, most vocations train people by holding up an ideal model, a standard by which all else is judged. For example, banks train new tellers by getting them to know the hallmarks of real money. Thus they learn to quickly recognize forgeries. We will use this same principle in our study of Israel. We will look to the Father's "gold standard" as we seek to define its perfect and ultimate representation—*the epitome of Israel.*

Jacob was first called "Israel" by the Almighty (Genesis 32:26-30). Jacob's sons, the Twelve Tribes of Israel, were his heirs—but they were soon divided into two houses. Then in Israel, a Son was born. He preferred to call Himself "the Son of Man," but He was a man with many names: *Immanuel, the Lamb of God, the Son of David, the Good Shepherd, the Glory of Israel,* to list only a few.

Paradoxically, incorrect interpretations of the life and death of the One called the Prince of Peace served to divide the people of Israel once again. Because of Him, another war began in Israel. It includes a fight for the title of "Israel." It is a conflict that has continued for almost 2000 years, pitting brother against brother. It is a battle that brings grief to the heart of our Heavenly Father.

Two groups of people today lay claim to the coveted title of Israel. Many adherents of Christianity and virtually all followers of Judaism believe themselves to be the true heirs of the patriarchs, and most deny the other the right to the title. So what is the truth? Who is Israel?

This question is crucial to our faith. Scripture mentions Israel some 2500 times, so our answers must not be vague. Also, "To them belongs the adoption as sons, the glory and the covenants, the giving of the Law, the temple service and the promises, whose are the fathers and from whom is the Messiah according to the flesh" (Romans 9:4-5). To be Israel is to be a prince who rules and reigns with the Almighty. So we ask, *who are these chosen people?*

For centuries the Church claimed the title of *New Israel* and thought they had replaced the *rejected* Jewish people. To them, ancient Israel became a mere teaching tool. Then, when modern Israel became a State in 1948, it caused an identity crisis: The God of Israel had aided the Jew in their return to His Land—and that made it difficult for the Church to continue to teach replacement theology.[8] Moreover, in the 1960's a new move began in the earth: Messianic Judaism. With it, Jewish Believers in the Messiah began to make their growing presence known, which likewise caused even more to ask, *"Who is Israel?"*

Traditionally, the most common responses to this crucial query have been:

- Jacob, whose name was changed to Israel
- The sons of Jacob—the Twelve Tribes
- The land given to the Twelve Tribes
- The Old Covenant people of the God of Israel
- The Ten Tribes of the Northern Kingdom
- The Church
- The Jewish people
- The present State of Israel

---

8 Islam teaches that both Jews and Christians were given God's truths but failed in their call, so He removed His favor from each, and the Muslims became the new "Chosen People." And, when Jesus returns, He will punish all non-Muslims (infidels).

The Israel Who Gathers Israel

The above list includes the most common responses to the Israel question. However, it does not include an "Israel" that stands head and shoulders above the rest. It leaves out the most important Israel of all. It fails to recognize the only One who is truly capable of being a Prince who rules with the Almighty. It leaves out Messiah Yeshua.

YHVH says "*Israel* is My son, My firstborn" (Exodus 4:22). In Isaiah we see an Israel who is appointed to "raise up the tribes of Jacob." That Son is none other than Messiah Yeshua, the Man with many names. In these verses we see both the Father and Yeshua speaking. The Father says, "Listen to Me, O islands [the nations]." Yeshua then says, "From the body of My mother He named Me. And He has made My mouth like a sharp sword... And He [YHVH] said to Me, 'You are My Servant, Israel, in Whom I will show My glory.' ...And now says YHVH who formed Me [Yeshua] from the womb to be His Servant, to bring Jacob back to Him, in order that Israel might be gathered to Him..., 'It is too small a thing that You should be My Servant to raise up the tribes of Jacob and to restore the preserved ones of Israel; I will also make You a light of the nations so that My salvation may reach to the end of the earth'" (Isaiah 49:1-6).

Yeshua fulfills these prophecies in numerous ways:

- Those of the "nations" were to listen to "the One named from the body of His mother."
  Our Heavenly Father named His Son "Yeshua" before He was born (Matthew 1:21).
- The One speaking has a mouth like a sharp sword.
  A sword is in Yeshua's mouth (Revelation 2:16).
- The Father calls this One, "My Servant, Israel."
  The Father calls Yeshua, "My Servant Whom I have chosen" (Matthew 12:18).

- Isaiah's Servant named Israel cannot be Jacob or his descendants because this Israel is destined to restore Jacob's tribes, to gather Jacob's scattered seed. *Our Messiah is the Good Shepherd who is restoring and regathering Israel's scattered and lost sheep (Psalm 23:3; Ezekiel 34:10-16; John 10:11-16; Matthew 15:24).*
- This Israel is said to be the One in whom the Father will show His glory. *When presented in the Temple as a firstborn son, Simeon said Yeshua was, "A light of revelation to the Gentiles, and the glory of Thy people Israel" (Luke 2:32). As that Light and Glory, Yeshua (whose name means Salvation), is causing the salvation of the God of Israel to reach to the ends of the earth.*

We also see that Yeshua is Israel in that the Father said, "Out of Egypt I called My son." Matthew, speaking of Yeshua's return from Egypt, says, "So was fulfilled what the Lord had said through the prophet: 'Out of Egypt I called My son'" (Hosea 11:1; Matthew 2:15). While the Hosea quote (from Exodus) applies to the Father bringing the sons of Israel out of Egypt, it also was fulfilled when He brought His only begotten Son, Yeshua/Israel, out of Egypt. Yeshua is the promised prophet like unto Moses (Deuteronomy 18:18-19; John 17:8,14,20; Acts 3:22-23). He is also the Servant/Israel through whom the sons of Israel are being regathered. The God of Israel says of Him, "It is too small a thing that You should be My Servant, to raise up the tribes of Jacob, and to restore the preserved ones of Israel. I will also make You a light of the nations so that My salvation may reach to the end of the earth." And, "I will appoint you as a covenant to the people, as a light to the nations, to open blind eyes, to bring out prisoners." And, "The people who walk in darkness will see a great light" (Isaiah 42:6-7; 9:2).

The Glorious Light of Israel

Yeshua came to fulfill what was spoken through Isaiah: "The land of Zebulun and the land of Naphtali, by the way of the sea, beyond the Jordan, Galilee of the Gentiles [these were former Ephraimite territories]—The people who were sitting in darkness saw a great light, to those who were sitting in the land and shadow of death, upon them a light dawned" (Matthew 4:14-16).

Messiah Yeshua said of Himself, "I am the light of the world, He who follows Me shall not walk in the darkness, but shall have the light of life...While I am in the world, I am the light of the world." In and through Messiah Yeshua and His people "the true Light is already shining" (John 8:12; 9:5; 1 John 2:8).

YHVH also has given our Messiah the throne of His father David. From it, He rules over the house of Jacob now and forever. He reigns over all who will submit to His rule, and He does so in a Kingdom that is without end. He has made purification for our sins and now sits at the right hand of the Majesty on High (Luke 1:32-33; Hebrews 1:3).

Yeshua's eternal Kingdom of Israel is both now, and yet to come.[9] In the same vein, He made a New Covenant with Israel that is both now and yet to come in its fullness. When we all know Him, and are no longer teaching neighbor and brother about YHVH, then, and only then, will we have entered into the fullness of Yeshua's New Covenant Kingdom (Jeremiah 31:31-33; Hebrews 8:8-12).

The Primary Player

To understand Israel, we must see that the primary player in the game is Messiah Yeshua. The Father is "summing up all things in Him" (Ephesians 1:10). He is bringing all things in heaven and on earth together under

---

9 Exo 19:6; 2 Sam 7:12-16; Dan 7:22; Luke 1:32-33; 12:32; Heb 1:3-8; 3:6; 8:1; 10:12-19; 12:2; 1 Pet 1:1; 2:5-10; Rev 3:21-22; 5:9-10; 20:6.

one head, Messiah. He is the appointed "heir of all things" (Hebrews 1:2). He is the *epitome*, the perfect prototype of all that the people of Israel are called to be.

If all teaching and leadership do not point to Yeshua, it points in the wrong direction. If it does not lift up Yeshua, it should not be lifted up. If we want to see Israel, we must look to and lift up Messiah Yeshua (John 12:32).

Israel: From Genesis to Revelation

Our God is called the God of Israel. The Bible is a book about the people of Israel. In the Book of Genesis our God names a man Israel. He then begins to call forth a people named Israel. In Revelation, Messiah Yeshua invites His people to come into the New Jerusalem and they must enter through gates named after the Twelve Tribes of Israel —because there are no other entrances.[10]

Scripture tells us that we will ultimately "name Israel's name with honor" (Isaiah 44:5). Textbooks declare, "In the Restoration, Israel's title will be a truth, not a misnomer."[11]

We need to walk in the full truth regarding both the houses of Israel. We need to see that our Father is still dealing with both Judah and Ephraim. And, in this hour, He seeks to make both of their sticks, *and their companions of Israel,* one stick in His hand (Isaiah 8:14; Ezekiel 37:15-28).

We also need to better understand the concepts of "Physical" and "Spiritual" Israel—because of the negative results that come from improper use of these designations.

Moreover, we need to see the difference in the different punishments and promises that were spoken over the two kingdoms of Israel—which two kingdoms are now on a decided collision course.

---

10 Rev 21:12; Eze 48:31.
11 *Theological Wordbook of the Old Testament*, Chicago, Moody Press, 1980, Vol. 1, # 997, p 444.

Three

Physical or Spiritual?

Messiah Yeshua said, "An hour is coming, and now is, when the true worshipers shall worship the Father in spirit and truth; for such people the Father seeks to be His worshipers" (John 4:23).

We live in that hour. We must be born from above of the Father's Holy Spirit and worship Him in spirit and in truth.

"Truth" is the Word, from Genesis to Revelation (Psalm 119:160; John 17:17). All Israel, Jew and non-Jew alike are called to worship the Father in spirit. Thus, in this sense we need to be "Spiritual Israel." However, to divide Israel into physical and spiritual camps insinuates that non-Jewish Believers do not descend from Abraham (which cannot be proven), and most importantly, it leads to separating the Church from Israel (which is not Scriptural).

Apart from Israel, the Church has no Covenant. Moreover, all of her members are "physical." Everyone who worships the Lord is physical and Israel is called to worship the Lord in spirit. Thus it is not good to use these designations to divide His people—especially in light of the preconceived notions and negative results associated with such divisions. Nonetheless, in light of the facts that many do divide Israel in this way, and since every Believer in Messiah is a physical being that descends from someone, our question becomes, *from whom do they descend?*

Abraham was promised *myriads* of biological offspring from his own loins. Logically, they should be found among Messiah's followers. He is Abraham's primary "Seed of Promise" and it seems reasonable that his numerous seeds would follow after Him (Genesis 15:1-6; Galatians 6:16).

While Believers are being built up into a "spiritual house," that should not be interpreted to mean that they are not possibly also biological seed. It especially should not lead to them being disinherited as part of greater Israel.

Being of the "spirit" is a sign that we have entered into Israel's New Covenant and belong to the Israel of God. Even if we do not descend from Abraham, in this physical life we belong to Messiah's eternal commonwealth of Israel. Beyond this important point, the fact is that YHVH's call for full repentance and full restoration of Israel is issued to both Ephraim and Judah "and their companions of Israel" (Isaiah 27:9; Ezekiel 37:15-19; Ephesians 2:11-22; 1 Peter 2:5).

We should not say that someone who is born from above is not of Israel. This leads Believers to separate themselves from Israel and to misunderstand their call. Non-Jewish Believers feel disconnected from (and thus become spiritual spectators to) the Father's plan for Israel when—according to Scripture—they should be active players in His game. Especially in these last days. It is critical for all Israel, both heirs and companions, to see their part in His great plan.

It is also essential that we adhere to the weightier matters of the spirit, but we must not neglect Yeshua's commandments concerning our earthly behavior either. He once said, "Woe to you, scribes and Pharisees, hypocrites! For you tithe mint and dill and cummin, and have neglected the weightier provisions of the law: justice and mercy and faithfulness; but these are the things you should have done without neglecting the others" (Matthew 23:23). We do not want to have the Messiah say to us, *"You kept the weightier matters, but should not have neglected the other things..."*

Four

Stumbling Ephraim and Judah

Blinded Ephraim[12] has misunderstood Yeshua in certain ways. Some think He did away with the "law." Unfortunately, they misunderstand His statement, "Do not think that I came to abolish the Law or the Prophets; I did not come to abolish but to fulfill" (Matthew 5:17). Yeshua came to *fulfill*, to *satisfy* the sacrificial requirements of the law.[13] He came to fully preach and perfect it, to personify how the Law is to be walked out. He "fulfilled" it by walking it out in all its glory. He showed us how it is to be done. However, this does not mean that He eliminated its eternal truths. Moreover, the Word says of the Messiah, "The one who says he abides in Him ought himself to walk in the same manner as He walked." As to how we are to walk as Believers, Messiah Yeshua said of His followers, "If you love Me, you will keep My commandments" (John 14:15; 1 John 2:6). Since this is the case, our next question naturally becomes, *what commandments does He want His New Covenant Believers to keep?*

---

12 Ephraim: See Definitions, pages iii-iv.
13 Fulfill: *Strong's* # G 4134. Rom 6:10; Heb 7:27; 9:12; 10:10;1 Pet 3:18; Jude 1:3.

As our sacrificial lamb, Yeshua was offered once for all, so we no longer need daily sacrifices. He is also our Yom Kippur offering (Hebrews 7:27; 9:7,12; 10:10; 1 Peter 3:18; Jude 1:3; 1 Corinthians 5:7). He fulfilled the requirements of the sacrificial system for us. In Him, we are no longer *under the curse* that comes from breaking the Law. However, the commandments of Torah that establish the principals of godly communal behavior continue to be *wisdom* to us. YHVH's laws make us stronger, healthier, and wiser when we reverence them: "You shall therefore keep every commandment...so that you may be strong and go in and possess the land [and]...prolong your days" (Deuteronomy 11:8-9).

The Torah, the Father's *loving instructions,* were given to help us succeed. It makes up the constitution of our nation. It tells of the history of our people. It reminds us of the glorious promises that YHVH gave to our forefathers. In its pages we find understanding. His Torah outlines a blessed life-style path that helps to keep us from all shame (1 John 4:8; 1 Kings 2:3; Deuteronomy 4:5-6; Psalm 119:1-6).

However, if we focus on the letter of its laws, if we seek eternal salvation by keeping its laws, we will fail. We will be found wanting. We must instead focus on the "spirit" of Torah and allow the *Ruach haKodesh* (the Holy Spirit) to write the Father's precious truths on our hearts. That is the very essence and goal of Israel's New Covenant.[14]

Torah teachers also must *nurture* the hearer. Mothers are the first to teach children and Proverbs tells us to listen to and not forsake our mother's *torah* (Proverbs 1:8; 6:20).[15] Mothers tend to deal with heart attitudes, which is foundational for all other Torah truths. This teaches us that the Father's Torah should *first* be presented to His children with a nurturing attitude.

---

14 Jer 31:31-33; Rom 3:23; Gal 3:10; Heb 8:10; 10:16. Also see, *Redeemed Israel,* chapter 28, "The Law and New Covenant Believers."
15 *Mama's Torah, The Role of Women,* Batya Wootten, 2004, 2010, Key of David Pub.

If a teaching is wrapped in legalism or cloaked in condemnation, it is not a true representation according to the Father's plan. Man criticizes and condemns. Abba's kind corrections include forgiveness and offer a solution to the problem (Romans 2:4; 2 Corinthians 7:9-10). It is our destiny to have the Father's Law written on our hearts by the Holy Spirit. The problem is not with His Law but with man's many misrepresentations of it.

Laws help us maintain order. Without them we have chaos, anarchy, and lawlessness. We must beware these attitudes because Yeshua said a day will come when He will say to those who practice lawlessness, "Depart from Me, I never knew you" (Matthew 7:21-23).

Some laws cannot be eliminated. Gravity is a law that we are forced to recognize. If we do something foolish and break its law we may die. If we likewise break the eternal Instructions of Torah we will suffer set consequences. This is not because our Heavenly Father waits eagerly to catch us in transgressions, but because His laws have automatic results. His laws work like the principle of sowing and reaping. For example, if we do not take a Sabbath rest every seventh day we risk having our bodies break down due to stress. Our God wants us to have a day in which we leave behind the cares of the world and turn to Him, to His love, and to focus on His provision for us. In this way we find both earthly and Heavenly rest in Him.[16]

Ephraim needs to learn to revere the eternal truths of Torah and no more regard its precepts as a "strange thing" (Hosea 8:12). As Believers, we are new creations in Messiah who are not under the curse of death that comes from breaking the law (2 Corinthians 5:17; Galatians 3:13). However, we desperately need to realize some greater truths about the One Whom We serve in spirit and truth. For He is, in truth, the Living Torah.

---

[16] *From Sabbath To Sunday*, S. Bacchiocchi, Maplewood NJ: Hammond, 1979, 2000.

Judah has a different problem in that they need to see the truth that Messiah Yeshua is somehow "One" with the Almighty Father. Yeshua, too, is our "*Elohim*," our God. He is the Father's unique and "Only Begotten Son," and yet, He cannot be a "lesser" God Who was later created (Isaiah 43:8-13; 44:8; John 1:14,18; 3:16,18).

Judah needs to realize that all Israel, including the Jewish people, need to be redeemed from their sins. Moreover, only a Divine *Elohim/God* can redeem our souls from *sheol*. Mortal man cannot do it. We are warned to "cease" trying to have a mere man do the job. Only God Himself can provide us with eternal redemption (Psalm 49:10,15).

This means, if Ephraim compromises on the truth about Yeshua's identity as *Elohim*, if he loses sight of the truth about our Redeemer, Ephraim will surely fail in his call, which is to help bring redemption to brother Judah.

Unfortunately, some Messianics have gotten tripped up in man-made legalisms as they are being drawn to return to Torah and to Israel's feasts. Because he tends to be jealous of Judah and his roots (Isaiah 11:13), Ephraim often seeks Judah's approval. To gain it, to feel that they "are part of Israel," many have denied faith in the Messiah and have converted to Judaism.

The problem is that Judah has been hardened to the truth of Messiah's Deity, so he tends to resist the very idea of a Divine Redeemer. Redeemed Israel must avoid these dangerous pitfalls. We must walk in the eternal truths of Torah while holding tightly to the hand of our Divine Redeemer.

There is much work to be done to bring all Israel into her fullness—but in and through Messiah Yeshua it can and will be done. To reunite Israel we look to the epitome of Israel. We look to Messiah Yeshua for eternal redemption and to see a proper Torah-based walk. When we walk as He walked, then the world will in truth see His Israel in action.

Five

Restoring Israel's Kingdom

I n our day, so to speak, we have two "kingdoms" of Israel: The Messiah's eternal Kingdom of Israel and the modern State of Israel. Moreover, these two houses/ kingdoms are now on a predetermined collision course.

Messiah Yeshua said His kingdom is "not of this world." Because He has already "sat down" at the right hand of the Almighty (Hebrews 1:1), He presently rules over His kingdom. His kingdom is both now and yet to come in all its fullness.[17] It is a kingdom that must first be established in our hearts. Flesh and blood cannot inherit it.

The subjects of Yeshua's kingdom are those who submit to Him. They are called to one day rule and reign with Him—but they are not to dominate in the flesh. They must instead serve in the spirit, even as He did.

To inherit this kingdom we must be re-born of the Spirit and worship our God in spirit and truth—and we must learn how to do so while sojourning here on earth, in earthly, fleshly bodies.

---

17 Yeshua presently rules over Israel's Kingdom. Ref, 1 Chr 14:2; 17:14; 28:5; 29:23; 2 Chr 9:8; 13:5,8; Isa 9:6-7; Luke 1:32-33; Eph 5:5; Heb 1:3; 3:6; 8:1; 10:12; John 18:36.

The Creator's mysterious yet simple pattern is, a seed is sown in a natural body and then raised in a spiritual body. It begins in the physical realm and culminates in the spiritual realm (1 Corinthians 15:36-50). To divide spiritual and physical Israel is equal to removing the germ from the seed. It cannot be done and would bring death rather than life.

YHVH made various covenants with His people, the most important one being Messiah's New Covenant. It offers unique and better promises—including removal (rather than covering) of sins, a changed heart/nature, and eternal life (Hebrews 12:24). *To simplify, it is having or not having Yeshua's New Covenant promise of eternal life that divides Israel.*

Yeshua's new covenant was made with physical Israelites. It includes a promise to restore David's Kingdom. To make this promise out to be other-worldly is to miss the mark. Yeshua will one day return to the Mount of Olives and Israel will reign with Him, by the Spirit, in this earth.[18]

So, asking who is Israel is equal to asking *who will rule with the Almighty?* For this reason some fight over the title— because they want to rule over others, to be preeminent, and to have power over others (1 Corinthians 4:7-8; Galatians 4:17). However, Messiah Yeshua said, "If anyone wants to be first, he shall be last of all, and servant of all."

To be Israel, one must be a servant of servants. Servant and Israel are inseparable concepts. Israel is forever chosen to choose—their choice is, to serve or not serve our God (Isaiah 44:21; 49:1-6; Mark 9:35). Israel also is a title that is given. In this life, men may temporarily take it for themselves, but in the end, it will be a name that the Almighty will bestow on His chosen ones. He alone will decide who meets His "Israel" standards. Israel also is a name given by the Father to His children, to His sons, and only He can disinherit a son. Brothers may want to do so, but it is not their prerogative (Exodus 4:22; Psalm 89:27; Jeremiah 31:9).

---

18 Jer 31:31-33; Mat 19:29; John 3:16; 5:24,39; 6:27-40; Acts 1:6-12; Heb 7:22; 8:6.

Our goal should be like that of Yeshua's Disciples. When He was about to ascend into Heaven, the last question they asked Him was, "Is it now that You are going to restore the Kingdom to Israel" (Acts 1:6). Their last question was not *if* He would do it, but *when* He would do it. It will happen. Yet, many have lost sight of the goal of the Messiah's Gospel —it being deliverance of the captives and restoration of Israel's Kingdom. He proclaimed *"the gospel of the kingdom."* To do so, He healed every kind of disease and sickness. And, He tells us, "This gospel of the kingdom shall be preached in the whole world as a testimony to all the nations, and then the end will come" (Matthew 4:23; 24:14). The end will not come *until* we learn to preach Messiah Yeshua's eternal "Gospel of the Kingdom."[19]

His Disciples shared this understanding. They said the outpouring of the Spirit on those of the Gentile nations was a sign that David's fallen booth/tabernacle/kingdom was being restored. They knew Israel had been scattered among the nations, and that YHVH had promised to raise up David's booth, to wall up its breaches, raise up its ruins and rebuild it as in days of old (Amos 9:11; Acts 15:13-18). We have lost sight of this precious end-time goal.

That happened to us for a reason and for a season, but now is the time for us to repent and return to Zion. Now is the time to work toward the full restoration of Messiah's glorious kingdom. Our focus has largely been on personal salvation, which is absolutely essential, but now we need to enlarge our tent, broaden our horizons and see the big picture. For, YHVH wants us to be a kingdom of priests.

Israel's High Priest wore an *ephod* with twelve stones on it that represented Israel's Twelve Tribes. This depicts the truth that the priest carried his brethren on his heart whenever he went into the Holy of Holies. We likewise need to care for, help, pray for, and lift up our beloved brothers.

---

19 The Kingdom Gospel: Psa147:2-4; Mat 9:35; Luke 16:16; Jhn 8:56; Gal 2:14; 3:8.

We must take no rest until they, too, have their inheritance (Joshua 1:12-15).

We need to learn to work together for the sake of the Kingdom. But let us realize that to work in *unison* is not equal to being *uniform* in our call. Each of us is unique and has a singular "row to hoe" in the Garden of Life. Yet, we need to plow in harmony, meaning we add to our particular call the idea of working toward our common goal: Restoration of Israel's Kingdom, preaching its Gospel.

The City of The Great King

We have a King and a Kingdom, and every kingdom has its capital city. Ours is the New Jerusalem, which will one day be centered on Mount Zion and called "The City of the Great King" (Psalm 48:2).

We are told to pray for earthly Jerusalem, that peace might be within her walls, prosperity within her palaces. Then we will prosper (Psalm 122:6,7). We pray for her because our Messiah loved her. He said, "O Jerusalem, Jerusalem...how often I wanted to gather your children together, just as a hen gathers her brood under her wings..." (Luke 13:34). We pray because Jerusalem is destined to become the "City of Truth." But the truth is, unless she acknowledges the Messiah as her King, she will never be any more than an old city with a lot of history.

We want to protect Jerusalem because she is Messiah's Bride. An angel said to John, "Come here, I will show you the bride, the wife of the Lamb." John then said, "[He] showed me the holy city, Jerusalem, coming down out of heaven....made ready as a bride adorned for her husband." And, "Blessed are those who are invited to the marriage supper of the Lamb." When Jerusalem comes down from Heaven, her sons then marry her (Isaiah 62:1-7; Revelation 21:2,9-10). So it is that watchmen are appointed to guard her, even as a bridegroom carefully watches over his bride.

Ephraim was called to be a watchman, to stand guard at his post and see what the Holy One would say to him (Isaiah 52:8; 62:6; Jeremiah 31:6; Hosea 9:8; Habakkuk 2:1). Ephraim is especially called to *shamar*, guard, protect, attend to, take heed, keep, mark, observe, preserve, be circumspect, regard, save, and thus, be a watchman.

YHVH says, "On your walls, O Jerusalem, I have set watchmen [*shomrim*]; all day and all night they will never keep silent. You who remind YHVH, take no rest for yourselves; and give Him no rest until He establishes and makes Jerusalem a praise in the earth" (Isaiah 62:6).[20]

We have a post to guard, a job to do. The problem is, the further away the Church gets from her Israelite roots, the more she tends to abandon this earthly post.

Many put great emphasis on being the bride of Messiah, but this can lead to wrong attitudes. We imagine ourselves as a bride because it teaches us the principles of purity. But we cannot focus on this point to the exclusion of other, equally important truths. Many types are used to teach us about our place in Messiah. We are His betrothed, His Body, Israel, the people of New Jerusalem, His watchmen, His bond-servants, etc. Seeing ourselves as all of these things, and not exclusively as an escaping bride, could help us better understand the end times.

Scenarios that depict Yeshua taking us away to a Heavenly wedding before New Jerusalem appears must be reexamined. Our job is to help establish her, *here*, on earth. We are told to pray, "Thy Kingdom come... *on earth.*"[21]

The days prior to instituting Yeshua's eternal Kingdom will be difficult but must not be *feared*. In them, we can know His protection and provision as we help restore His Kingdom. Just as the ancient flood waters drowned many, those same waters buoyed up Noah and his family and carried them to safety. Just as there was darkness in Egypt

---

20 *Shamar: S&BDB* # H 8104; *Tsaphah:* # H 6822; Watch: # H 4931.
21 Dan 7:18; Mic 4:8; Mat 6:10; 12:28.

during the time of judgment, so there was light in the land of Goshen. The cloud and fire that confounded the pursuing Egyptians provided protection and gave guidance to the sons of Israel. The fire that burned Nebuchadnezzar's mighty men loosed the bonds of Shadrach, Meshach, and Abed-nego. Saints sometimes must go through fire, or even be "baptized with fire" (Luke 3:16-17). Such fire is a terror to those that do not know Him, but for those who do know Him, it purges our dross and leaves us purified.[22]

We must not put inordinate focus on judgments that are decreed for the wicked. As YHVH's "preserved ones" we must focus on His good plan for us (Isaiah 49:1-6). We want to focus on being faithful—if need be, even unto death. [23]

As for guarding our post, we have been misled concerning Judah's salvation. *They will not see Yeshua until they first call Him the Blessed One.* John applied Zechariah's prophecy about beholding a "pierced" Messiah to Yeshua's crucifixion. And, He said to Judah, "You will not see me again *until you say, 'Blessed is He who comes in the name of the* LORD'" (Zechariah 12:10; John 19:37; Matthew 23:37-39).

Judah believes and then he sees. And, the non-Jew is supposed to provoke Judah to that faith! (Romans 11). Change must first come to Ephraim. Judah will believe when he see Ephraim truly representing the Messiah, the Spirit, and Torah. The plan is not for us to leave brother Judah, but, like our forefather, Joseph, we need to be a help in time of need. [24]

Nonetheless, the focus of many is on the various "rapture" theories—the timing of which is hotly debated. But, what is the outcome of such study? Does it encourage us to work to rebuild Israel's Kingdom, and not love our lives even unto death (Proverbs 2:21-22; Revelation 12:11). Or, does it encourage us to fearfully look for an escape?

---

22 *The Feasts of the Lord,* Robert Thompson, Medford, OR: Omega Pub., 1975, p 139. *Do Not Fear:* Jer 46:28; Zec 8:13-15; Mat 10:26-31; Luke 12:7,32; 1 Pet 3:14; Rev 2:10.
23 *Restoring Israel's Kingdom,* A. Wootten, 2000, 2010, Key of David Publishing.
24 See *Redeemed Israel* by Batya Wootten, chapter 26, "The Two Witnesses."

Scripture	Restored Israel Hallmarks
Isaiah 11:13	Ephraim's jealousy departs
Jeremiah 31:18,19	Ephraim repents of his paganism
Isaiah 11:13	Those hostile to Judah are cut off
Isaiah 11:13	Judah ceases to vex Ephraim
Zechariah 10:7	Ephraim becomes like a mighty man
Hosea 11:10	Ephraim comes trembling from the West
Zechariah 10:8,10	Ephraim returns in great numbers
Obadiah 1:18	Jacob becomes a fire, Joseph a flame
Zechariah 9:13	Judah is like a bow, Ephraim the arrow
Jeremiah 3:14; 50:5	Repentant Israel asks for the way to Zion
Jeremiah 50:20	No more iniquity found in Israel
Jeremiah 3:17;16:14	Both forget the Ark and the Exodus
Zechariah 8:3,7,13	Both call Zion "The City of Truth"
Ezekiel 37:15-28	Two sticks become one nation in the land
Ezekiel 37:24	Ephraim & Judah have one King—Yeshua
Ezekiel 37:23-24	Not defiled with any transgressions
Ezekiel 37:26-27	YHVH's sanctuary is in their midst forever

Until the above verses are completely fulfilled
the Father is still working with both the houses of Israel.
Ephraim and Judah have not been fully reunited—
our unity has been imputed in the Messiah,
but we have not fully implemented that unity.
Copyright © 2006-2010, Batya Ruth Wootten

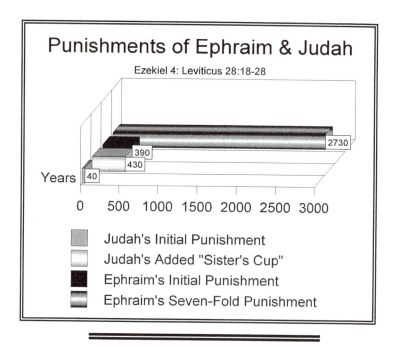

Punishments of Ephraim & Judah

Ezekiel 4: Leviticus 28:18-28

2730
390
430
40

Years

0   500   1000 1500 2000 2500 3000

Judah's Initial Punishment
Judah's Added "Sister's Cup"
Ephraim's Initial Punishment
Ephraim's Seven-Fold Punishment

In Ezekiel we see that both Ephraim and Judah were given certain punishments for their idolatry. However, in addition to her 40 years, Judah also had to "drink her sister's cup" for an additional 390-year penalty. This gave Judah a total of 430 years of punishment, which began when their capital, Jerusalem, became a vassal city of Babylon. Judah lost their political control around 595 B.C. Their punishment came to an end in 166 B.C. with the cleansing of the Temple by the Maccabees.

On the other hand, Ephraim did not repent of her idolatries, so her 390-year punishment was increased sevenfold, resulting in a total of 2730 years in which she would be "Not a people," even as Hosea prophesied (vs. 1:9). Ephraim's cities slowly became vassal cities of conquering Assyria starting around 734 B.C. She lost her capital, Samaria, and went into captivity in 722 B.C. Thus, her "Not a people" punishment ended around 1996. Now, she is being restored to her Israelite roots and heritage.

For more information concerning these punishments, see the book, *Restoring Israel's Kingdom* by Angus Wootten, 2000, 2010, Key of David Publishing, Saint Cloud, FL.

Six

A Door of Hope
For The Last Days

D ays are coming that will prove to be dark for the disobedient. However, they can prove to be days of light and glory for Messiah's followers (Psalm 91:7).

Many agree that trouble is coming, but Christianity's primary question seems to be, *"When will we escape? When will we be 'raptured,' taken away to be with the Lord?"*[25] They assume that they will not have to suffer in what is known as "The Great Tribulation, or "Jacob's Trouble," or "The Wrath,"[26] but will instead be *translated*, or *raptured*, to go and be with the Lord. The proposed timing of this *supposed* earthly removal falls into several broad categories:

- Pre-Tribulation Rapture (before the seven-year period described in Daniel 9 starts)
- Mid-Tribulation Rapture (3 ½ year, midway point)
- Pre-Wrath Rapture (before God's wrath is poured out, generally thought to be after the midway point)
- Post-Tribulation Rapture (raptured at the end).[27]

---

25 *Raptured Onto the Back of a Horse* by Batya Wootten examines these theories.
26 See Jer 30:7; Zep 1:15; Mat 24:21.
27 "This doctrine holds that there is a Resurrection-Rapture of living believers in
(continued...)

The various rapture theories are rooted in the following collective ideas: Believers will be "caught up" in the air to meet the Lord; there will a period of tribulation; which is followed by a Millennial Reign, in which the Messiah will rule for a thousand years before eternity begins (Daniel 9:27; 1 Thessalonians 4:15-17; Revelation 20:1-6).

These theories are not well received in nations where Believers are put to death for their faith. They reject them because they intimately know persecution's pains. They do not regard the almost exclusively western idea of "insulation" from testing as being a valid end-time view. They know that we are to take up our "cross," and pass through "many tribulations" before entering into God's kingdom—and that we gain patient endurance by not loving our lives, even on pain of death (Matthew 10:38; Acts 14:22; Revelation 13:10).[28]

Messiah said we would have tribulation, perhaps be imprisoned, tested, and even put to death. Throughout history, Believers have been tortured and killed by the enemy. So we should expect some tribulation in life.[29]

The late Corrie Ten Boom was a Christian woman who lost most of her family in the Holocaust because they hid Jewish people in their home. Afterward, she often cautioned Believers saying, "The rapture -before-tribulation doctrine is now an exclusively American message." This woman of truly tested faith repeatedly warned all who had ears to hear, *"Don't listen to those false prophets..."*[30]

---

27 (...continued)
Jesus Christ at the end of the age (or the 'End times'). Post-tribulationists believe that Christians will remain on the Earth through the seven year tribulation period, to be gathered by the angels to meet Christ in the air (raptured) at Christ's second coming and then return with Him as Christ descends to the Earth, to usher in the millennium on earth. This is usually understood as being in line with historic pre-millennialism" (http://en.wikipedia.org/wiki/Post_Tribulation_Rapture).

28 Luke 21:19; 2 Cor 6:4; Heb 10:36; 12:1; James 1:3-4; 5:11.

29 John 16:33; Rom 8:35; 2 Cor 1:4; Heb 11:37; Rev 2:10.

30 Corrie Ten Boom: *The Hiding Place*, Elizabeth Sherrill, Chosen Books, 1996. The late Ruth Graham likewise spoke against the theory: www.tribulationcentral.com

Teachings about the Rapture can degenerate into a form of escapism. If we tell people they will escape trouble and it comes upon them, it will shake their faith and even set them up for the "falling away" that comes prior to the man of sin being revealed (2 Thessalonians 2:3). We must not focus on avoiding momentary earthly affliction but set our sights on the transcendent eternal reward that awaits all who show unfailing allegiance during the end-times. Those who are "beheaded because of the testimony of Yeshua, and because of the word of God…will be priests of God… and will reign with Him" (Revelation 20:4-6).[31]

We must not concentrate on the punishments of the unrighteous while neglecting to study the glorious promises that await the righteous. We should not focus on the penalties that come from breaking His laws or but on the blessings He bestows on Believers. We need to trust that He will not test us beyond what we are able to bear—and that, with every test, He provides the power to endure. Fear paralyzes. If we focus on fearful things we become inanimate, fruitless, and frozen with fear. If we obey and instead focus on YHVH's promises of life and deliverance, we are inspired, we become animated, spirited, and full of life!Again, while there was darkness in Egypt there was light in Goshen. So let us focus on the Light![32]

The actual timing of the rapture—when mortality puts on immortality—when Believers who are alive at His coming are transformed bodily—is a hotly debated subject that we cannot properly address in this limited work.[33] However, regardless of when that transformation does take place, regardless of how long we might have to stay in a war-torn earth, we suggest everyone adopt the following attitude:

---

31 Rev 20:4,6; 22:12; John 15:13; Luke 6:23.
32 Jer 46:28; Zec 8:13-15; Mat 10:26-31; Luke 12:7,32; 1 Cor 10:13; 1 Thes 5:5; 1 Pet 3:14; Rev 2:10.
33 See Hosea 13:14; 1 Cor 15:50-55; 1 Thes 4:16-17, and the forthcoming book, *Raptured Onto the Back of a Horse* by Batya Wootten, Key of David Pub.

*It is better for us to be prepared and not called upon than to **not** be prepared and be called upon.*

Let us therefore prepare our hearts, set our faces, and determine that, to be best or our ability, we will follow our Messiah wherever He might choose to lead us, and for however long He might deem that we should remain on this earth. As instructed, we will seek to occupy until He returns! (Luke 19:13).

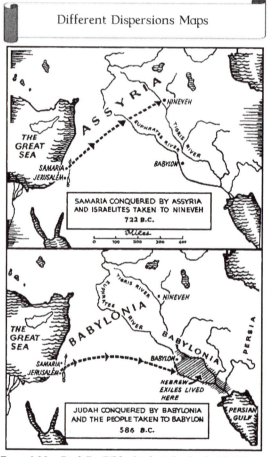

Different Dispersions Maps

SAMARIA CONQUERED BY ASSYRIA AND ISRAELITES TAKEN TO NINEVEH 722 B.C.

JUDAH CONQUERED BY BABYLONIA AND THE PEOPLE TAKEN TO BABYLON 586 B.C.

From *A Map Book For Bible Students* by Frederick L. Fay, page 18, Old Tappan, NJ: Fleming H. Revell. Used by permission.

Seven

Our Glorious Future

The Father has a glorious future planned for an obedient Ephraim and Judah. However, even as our Messiah suffered, some of us may have to suffer for His cause, but in the end, even as He has been glorified, so will we be glorified. We see His future promises of glory when we examine some of Israel's as-yet unfulfilled prophecies.

The following chapter lists some of these awesome promises. With minor changes, the text is essentially taken from the book, *Redeemed Israel—Reunited and Restored*.

We quote from chapter 30, "An Israel Yet to Come"—

Just as King David once ruled over all Israel, so too will Messiah Yeshua one day be King over all Israel:

"'At that time,' declares YHVH, 'I will be the God of all the families of Israel, and they shall be My people'" (Jeremiah 31:1; ref 33:24).

"The sons of Israel will come, both they and the sons of Judah as well; they will go along weeping as they go, and it will be YHVH their God that they seek. They will ask for the way to Zion, turning their faces in its direction; they will come that they may join themselves to YHVH" (Jeremiah 50:4-5).

When YHVH fully reunites both the houses of Israel, they will reach out to one another in true forgiveness and humility. Then, "the house of Judah will [again] walk with the house of Israel." And, "In those days ten men from all the nations will grasp the garment of a Jew saying, 'Let us go with you, for we have heard that God is with you'" (Jeremiah 3:18; 33:24; Zechariah 8:23).

Ten to one was the ratio used when the Father gave Jeroboam ten of Israel's tribes (1 Kings 11:31,36).[34] Ephraim out-numbered Judah ten to one: "The sons of Israel were 300,000, and the men of Judah 30,000" (1 Samuel 11:8). While Ephraim has grabbed hold of the garment (*tzit-tzit: fringe*) of the Lion of Judah, Yeshua, they will also grab hold of their brother, Judah, and the two houses of Israel will then join forces. "In that day the nations will resort to the root of Jesse...then it will happen on that day that YHVH will again recover the second time with His hand the remnant of His people....And He will lift up a standard for the nations, and will assemble the banished ones of Israel, and will gather the dispersed of Judah from the four corners of the earth" (Isaiah 11:10-12). "At that time, they shall call Jerusalem 'The Throne of YHVH'" (Jeremiah 3:17).

Our Father will gather Judah and Israel.[35] Formerly divided brothers will begin to honor one another, and to collectively honor the godly things each has accomplished in the earth through YHVH's anointing (Romans 13:7).

Trembling Ephraim Will Be Gathered

We have already begun to see the miracle of the regathering of Judah, but we have not yet seen the fulfillment of YHVH's glorious plan to re-gather scattered Ephraim. And gather him He will, for Abba said of them,

---

34 Jeroboam later became the first king of Israel's Northern Kingdom (1 Ki 12:20).
35 The *NIV Study Bible*, Zondervan, 1995, says: "In the Messianic age God's divided people will again be united (see e.g., Isa 11:12; Eze 37:15-23; Hos 1:11)," Jer 3:18, p 1119.

"How can I give you up, O Ephraim? How can I surrender you, O Israel?... All My compassions are kindled...I will not destroy Ephraim again....They will walk after YHVH, He will roar like a lion; indeed He will roar, and His sons will come trembling from the west" (Hosea 11:8-10).

While scattered, Ephraim will be instructed and begin to see the glorious truth about his heritage (Jeremiah 31:18-19). He will also begin to see the many ways in which he has offended his God through his past actions. This will cause him to tremble in fear and hasten to correct his mistakes. He will perceive the awesomeness of his God as well as His glorious plan for His restored people and will then become a "vessel fit for honorable use" (Hosea 8:8; Romans 9:21-23).[36] Made ready to walk in the footsteps of his father Joseph, Ephraim will become a source of protection and provision for his family. Then will the Father whistle for him to return to His Land (Zechariah 10:8).

Where Did They All Come From?

Isaiah speaks cryptically of Israel's coming reunion: "Shout for joy, O heavens! And rejoice, O earth! Break forth into joyful shouting, O mountains! For YHVH has comforted His people and will have compassion on His afflicted." In response, troubled Judah says, "The LORD has forsaken me, and *Adonai* has forgotten me."[37]

Abba answers Judah's cry, saying, "Can a woman forget her nursing child and have no compassion on the son of her womb? Even these may forget, but I will not forget you. 'Behold, I have inscribed you on the palms of My hands; your walls are continually before Me. Your builders hurry; your destroyers and devastators will depart from you. 'Lift up your eyes and look around; all of them gather

---

36 Tremble/*charad*: S&BDB # H 2729.

37 *Adonai*: S&BDB # H 136. Form of H 113; (used as a name for God). *My Lord*; especially used by the house of Judah to speak of the Almighty One.

together, they come to you. As I live,' declares YHVH, 'You will surely put on all of them as jewels and bind them on as a bride. For your waste and desolate places and your destroyed land—surely now you will be too cramped for the inhabitants, and those who swallowed you will be far away. The children of whom you [Zion, once the capital of a united house of Israel] were bereaved will yet say in your ears, 'The place is too cramped for me; make room for me that I may live here.' Then you [Judah] will say in your heart, 'Who has begotten these for me, since I have been bereaved of my children and am barren, an exile and a wanderer? And who has reared these? Behold, I was left alone; from where did these come?" To this the Father responds, "Behold, I will lift up My hand to the nations and set up My standard to the peoples; and they will bring your sons in their bosom, and your daughters will be carried on their shoulders" (Isaiah 49:13-23).

Ephraim will yet return to his homeland and he will happily bring those of Judah with him.[38]

The Two Sticks

The Father speaks of uniting the two families of Israel when uniting the "two sticks" that represent them. Of that day the Holy One said to Ezekiel:

"'Son of man, take for yourself one stick and write on it, 'For Judah and for the sons of Israel, his companions;' then take another stick and write on it, 'For Joseph, the stick of Ephraim and all the house of Israel, his companions.' Then join them for yourself one to another into one stick, that they may become one in your hand.

"And when the sons of your people speak to you saying; 'Will you not declare to us what you mean by these?' say to

---

38 In Hebrew *dalet* means door. YHVH's Name is spelled יהוה. Judah means praise and is spelled like YHVH with a dalet added, יהודה. Praise is the door to YHVH, Yeshua is the Door and He came through the tribe of Judah (John 10:7-9; Rev 3:20).

them, 'Thus says YHVH Elohim,' 'Behold, I will take the stick of Joseph, which is in the hand of Ephraim, and the tribes of Israel, his companions; and I will put them with it, with the stick of Judah, and make them one stick, and they will be one in My hand....I will take the sons of Israel from among the nations where they have gone, and I will gather them from every side and bring them into their own land; and I will make them one nation in the land, on the mountains of Israel; and one king will be king for all of them; and they will no longer be two nations, and they will no longer be divided into two kingdoms. And they will no longer defile themselves with their idols, or with their detestable things, or with any of their transgressions....And they will be My people, and I will be their God....They will all have one shepherd...and I will...set My sanctuary in their midst forever. My dwelling place also will be with them; and I will be their God, and they will be My people'" (Ezekiel 37:16-27).

Ezekiel said this "Son of man" would join two sticks together. Yeshua called Himself the "Son of Man" and one day He took up "two sticks" that were joined together in the form of a cross. He hung on those two sticks (or tree branches) so Jewish and non-Jewish Israel could become one new man. At the foot of His cross, by His spirit, we learn to become Israel redeemed, reunited, and restored.

As worthy servants, let each of us therefore take up our cross, let us take up the tests that come into our lives, and follow Messiah. Let us also explain to the world the meaning and call to unity that is found in the finished work of His "two sticks."[39]

An Invincible Army

When Ephraim and Judah are reunited in YHVH

---

[39] Thanks to Dani'el Holmes of St. Louis for sharing the point about the cross being "two sticks." See Eze 37:16; Mat 9:6; 10:38; 12:8,40; 16:24; 17:22; 18:11; Luke 9:23. Sticks/Trees: S&BDB # H 6086: 'ets, ates; from H 6095; a tree.

Elohim, when their reunion is fully manifested, they become an invincible army of powerful, prevailing princes capable of fighting the battles of the God of Israel.

The *Amplified Bible* says of this coming army, "But [with united forces] Ephraim and Judah will swoop down upon the shoulder of the Philistines land sloping toward the west; together they will strip the people on the east... They will lay their hand upon Edom and Moab, and the Ammonites shall obey them" (Isaiah 11:14).

Of that glorious day, YHVH says:

"I will bend Judah as My bow, I will fill the bow with Ephraim....Then YHVH will appear over them...and YHVH will blow the trumpet...YHVH Tsa'va'ot will defend them...He will save them in that day as the flock of His people; for they are as the stones of a crown, sparkling in His land...For YHVH of hosts has visited His flock, the house of Judah, and will make them like His majestic horse in battle...and they will be as mighty men, treading down the enemy in the mire of the streets in battle; and they will fight, for YHVH will be with them; and the riders on horses will be put to shame. And I shall strengthen the house of Judah, and I shall save the house of Joseph... Ephraim will be like a mighty man, and their heart will be glad as if from wine; indeed, their children will see it and be glad, their heart will rejoice in YHVH.

"I will whistle for them to gather them together, for I have redeemed them; and they will be as numerous as they were before...They will remember Me in far countries, and they with their children will live and come back. I will bring them back from the land of Egypt, and gather them from Assyria; and I will bring them into the land of Gilead and Lebanon, until no room can be found for them... The sons of Judah and the sons of Israel will be gathered together," and their reunion will be glorious, "For great will be the day of Jezreel" (Zechariah 9:13-10:10; Hosea 1:11).

A Day of Holiness

Great and holy will be the day when the Father fully reunites His chosen people, for He has sworn: "All the sinners of my people will die by the sword." And, "'It will come about in that day... that I will cut off the names of the idols from the land, and they will no longer be remembered; and I will also remove the prophets and the unclean spirit from the land.' And, "I will remove from your midst your proud, exulting ones. And you will never again be haughty on My holy mountain. But I will leave among you a humble and lowly people, and they will take refuge in the name of YHVH. The remnant of Israel will do no wrong and tell no lies, nor will a deceitful tongue be found in their mouths" (Amos 9:10; Zechariah 13:2; Zephaniah 3:11-13).

The Father will yet have His way. He will have an obedient, united House of Israel. He will have a House of Israel that loves Him, His people, and His Messiah.

A Collision Course

At this time in history, the people of Israel and the eternal Kingdom of Israel, are on a collision course. Long ago the Almighty made a promise to our father Abraham; that promise essentially included a piece of real estate and the promise to bless and multiply Abraham's seed. Then came Messiah Yeshua. In and through Him, Israel received a new and much better covenant. The gift of eternal life is promised to all who enter into this covenant and believe in the Messiah and in His sacrifice in our behalf. The ability to be reborn from above and become an eternal son of the Living God is the gift that is freely given to us.[40]

Messiah Yeshua was given the throne of his forefather, David, and He was promised that His would be a kingdom that is without end. It is a kingdom that is not of this world,

---

40 Jer 31:31-33; Hos 1:10; Heb 7:22; 8:6-13; 9:15; 12:24; Luke 1:31-33; Isa 9:6-7; Rom 9:26; Eph 2:8; John 3:7; 6:54; 18:36.

it is one that is now and is yet to come. It also is a kingdom that must ever be alive in our hearts.[41]

Similarly, the chosen city, Jerusalem, the City of Gold, the City of the Great King, stands naked when separated from the glory of her Messiah. She and her people are destined to be married.[42] To lose sight of the New Covenant gift of eternal life that is promised to all who follow the Messiah into this glorious City is to be short-sighted about the primary promise made to the chosen people. It is to fail to seek after the very thing for which father Abraham so earnestly sought: "For he was looking for the city which has foundations, whose architect and builder is God" (Hebrews 11:10).

To lose sight of Jerusalem's full restoration in Messiah is to have a limited view of Israel's promised Kingdom, it is to see Israel in part. If we are going to catch a vision of Israel we must see that Israelites can be Israelites and fail to see the truth about the restoration of Messiah's Yeshua's Kingdom; they also can participate in the earthly promises given to our patriarchs, and even live in the Promised Land and be multiplied, yet miss seeing the all-important gift of eternal life that is found in our Messiah.

Faith in Messiah Yeshua, or a lack thereof, is what separates Israel. Obedient Israel is destined to belong to both the King and His Kingdom of Israel. But woe to those who cause others to stumble over Him because they have misrepresented Him to their brethren. He spoke of a father who had two sons who he asked to go and work in his vineyard. One son promised to go, but did not. The other refused to go, but then went and did his father's bidding. The moral of the story is that neither son did a perfect job.

---

41 2 Sam 7:12-16; Psa 89:3-4,26-29, 36-37.

42 That Yeshua has already "sat down" indicates that He now rules over His kingdom (Luke 1:32; Heb 1:3; 10:12; 12:2; Rev 3:21). His kingdom is yet to come in its fullness: Matt 6:10; Luke 11:2; also see Isa 27:9; 55:3; 59:21; Jer 31:31-34; 32:38-40; Heb 8:8-12; 10:16. Jerusalem: Isa 62:1-7; Rev 21:2,9-10; Psa 48:1-2; Mat 5:35.

Both failed their father on some level (Matthew 21:28-32). And in the same vein, both of us, both Ephraim and Judah have failed our Heavenly Father in the past. But, now is the time for us to weep in true repentance, to lock arms, and together, go and do work in our Father's vineyard. Together, we need to become the obedient and glorious reunited Israel of whom our prophets spoke.

The Answer to the Question

One day soon, the sky will part, and a glorious Messiah Yeshua will be revealed. Seated on a white horse, the Prince who is *Yisrael*, will sit tall in His saddle. In that day, Yeshua will be clothed in a robe dipped in blood, and will have written on His thigh a title:

King of Kings and LORD *of Lords.*

He also will have in His hand a scepter of two sticks that have been made one in His hand. In that moment, the whole world will behold His glory. He will then nudge His steed to move toward the Earth. In that instant, all who are His will be changed. The mortals who love Him will instantly become immortal. In the twinkling of an eye, a redeemed people will find themselves seated on white horses. They will have been prepared to forever serve their Master. They have been made ready to return and reign with their King. In that awesome moment, the answer to the *who is Israel* question, will be finally and forever answered.

May we, by His grace, prove to be part of that answer. May we prove to be part of Yeshua's redeemed people, Yisràel. When He returns, may He find us working toward the reunification and restoration of His eternal Kingdom.

Holy One of Israel, we pray, may Thy Kingdom come, Thy will be done, on Earth, as it is in Heaven.

Amen and Amen. So be it.

Fall and Restoration of Israel's Kingdom

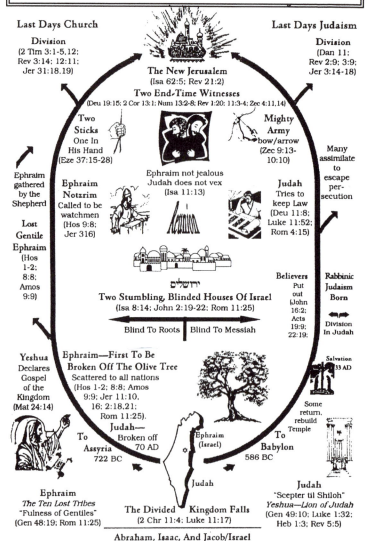

Last Days Church

Division
(2 Tim 3:1-5,12;
Rev 3:14; 12:11;
Jer 31:18,19)

Last Days Judaism

Division
(Dan 11;
Rev 2:9; 3:9;
Jer 3:14-18)

The New Jerusalem
(Isa 62:5; Rev 21:2)

Two End-Time Witnesses
(Deu 19:15; 2 Cor 13:1; Num 13:2-8; Rev 1:20; 11:3-4; Zec 4:11,14)

Two Sticks
One In
His Hand
(Eze 37:15-28)

Mighty Army
bow/arrow
(Zec 9:13-
10:10)

Ephraim
gathered
by the
Shepherd

Many assimilate to escape persecution

Lost Gentile Ephraim
(Hos
1-2;
8:8;
Amos
9:9)

Ephraim Notzrim
Called to be
watchmen
(Hos 9:8;
Jer 316)

Ephraim not jealous
Judah does not vex
(Isa 11:13)

Judah
Tries to
keep Law
(Deu 11:8;
Luke 11:52;
Rom 4:15)

יהושלים

Two Stumbling, Blinded Houses Of Israel
(Isa 8:14; John 2:19-22; Rom 11:25)

Blind To Roots   Blind To Messiah

**Believers
Put
out**
(John
16:2;
Acts
19:9;
22:19:

Rabbinic Judaism Born

Division
In Judah

**Yeshua
Declares
Gospel
of the
Kingdom**
(Mat 24:14)

**Ephraim—First To Be
Broken Off The Olive Tree**
Scattered to all nations
(Hos 1-2; 8:8; Amos
9:9; Jer 11:10,
16; 2:18,21;
Rom 11:25).

**Salvation
33 AD**

Judah—
Broken off
70 AD

To
Assyria
722 BC

Ephraim
(Israel)

To
Babylon
586 BC

Some
return,
rebuild
Temple

Judah

Ephraim
The Ten Lost Tribes
"Fulness of Gentiles"
(Gen 48:19; Rom 11:25)

The Divided   Kingdom Falls
(2 Chr 11:4; Luke 11:17)

Judah
"Scepter til Shiloh"
Yeshua—Lion of Judah
(Gen 49:10; Luke 1:32;
Heb 1:3; Rev 5:5)

Abraham, Isaac, And Jacob/Israel
Father of a Multitude—Joint Heirs
(Gen 26:3; 28:4; 1 Chr 16:16-17; Heb 11:9,39,40; Gal 3:29)

Eight

Twelve Tips About Twelve Tribes

T he following chapters can be used as an outline in a personal or group Bible study. For groups, have the leader read aloud the outline statement, have others read aloud the Scripture references, then discuss them. The Word will speak for itself and come alive with new meaning concerning Israel and the Believer.

1) Abraham was promised that *myriads* of descendants would come from his *loins*. This does not mean one has to be an actual descendant to share in his faith, but that we should view the incredible promise that YHVH made to him in proper context (Gen 15:1-6; 24:60; 26:4; 28:3,4; 28:14).[43]

2) Abraham, Isaac, and Jacob/Israel were joint heirs of the same promise (Gen 15:5; 17:4; 26:3-4; 24:60; 28:3,4,14; 48:4,16,19; 1 Chr 16:16-17; Heb 11:9).

3) Like the United States, Israel was divided into Northern and Southern Kingdoms—by the Almighty—and their two houses have never been fully reunited. He makes their two sticks one stick in His hand in the last days (1 Ki 12:24; Isa 11:14; Jer 3:14-18; Ezek 37:15-28; Zec 8:3-13; 10:7-10).

---

43 Myriads: See *Strong's Concordance* word #'s H 505 and 7235.

4) When YHVH makes the "two sticks" described in Ezekiel, "one stick in His hand," three things happen: Israel will no longer be plucked up from the Land, will no longer defile themselves with any of their transgressions, and they will have one king—the King of Kings and Lord of Lords. A fully reunited Israel is a blameless Israel that lives forever under Messiah's rule in the Land of Promise (Eze 37:15-28).

5) Scripture calls these two kingdoms, "both the houses of Israel," YHVH's "two nations," and "the two families that YHVH chose" (Isa 8:14; Jer 33:23-26; Eze 35:10; 37:22).

6) Those of Ephraim, the Northern Kingdom of Israel, were scattered among *every* nation. Through this scattering, they were destined to become a *"melo hagoyim,"* a "fullness of the Gentiles" (Hos 1-2; 8:8; Amos 9:9; Rom 11).

7) The gifts and calling of God are without repentance. Thus, there is an eternal call on all Israel, both Judah and Ephraim. Both are called to love and obey YHVH with all their heart (Deu 28:1-6; Num 23: 19; Isa 43:10; Rom 11:29).

8) Once scattered among the nations, the Ephraimites became degenerate and wild olive branches. When they are grafted back in to the Root of the Tree (Messiah Yeshua), they are supposed to learn to walk in a way that provokes those of Judah (make them jealous of Ephraim's living relationship with the Holy One), and thus make Judah want what Ephraim has (Isa 35:10; Jer 11: 10,16; 2:18, 21; 9:26; Eze 37:16; Hos 1:9,1; Rom 11).

9) Non-Jewish Believers in Messiah also are full heirs of Abraham's promise and share full citizenship in Messiah's eternal commonwealth of Israel (Gen 17:4-7; Isa 56:5; Eze 47:23; Rom 4:17; Eph 2:11-22; Gal 3:29).

10) The Father decreed a perpetual statute regarding sojourners. When they abide by His three proscribed citizenship rules they must thereafter be regarded as a native of the Land, they are no longer Gentiles or heathen. The three rules are: observance of Passover, circumcision, and sojourn (live in harmony) with His chosen people (Exo 12:48; Lev 19:34; Num 9: 14; Isa 56:3; Eph 2:11-19). These rules were continued in Messiah Yeshua's commonwealth (see page 49 for many Scripture references).

11) While on Earth, Jews and Christians—Judah and Ephraim—are called to serve as two witnesses for the God of Israel. Their divine purpose is to confirm the truth of His Holy Word, from beginning to end, Genesis to Revelation (Num 35:30; Deu 17:6; 19:15; John 8:17; 2 Cor 13:1).

12) Romans 11:25 reveals that the truth about all Israel was destined to be a "mystery" until the "fullness of Gentiles," the *"melo hagoyim"* promised to Ephraim, "be come in." This *fullness* can speak of a given number—or of *maturation.* [44] If the latter meaning was intended, this verse has to do with Ephraim "growing up." It has to do with them being properly instructed and thus coming to know themselves as part of the people of Israel. (Heb 6:1-17). It has to do with great change coming to Ephraim! The veil is being lifted in these last days. All Israel is coming to understand the formerly hidden truth about the partial hardening of both houses of Israel—Judah and Ephraim (Rom 11:25; Gen 48:19; Jer 31:18,19).

"Genetic Memory" seems to direct Monarch butterflies in their annual and, *with each fourth generation,* completely unknown, migratory paths. Perhaps the LORD is likewise turning on a genetic memory in Believers the world over.[45] They feel inexplicably drawn to Israel, the Feasts, the truths of Torah, Judah, and the Promised Land. With this drawing we might be seeing a *predisposed* returning Ephraim!

---

44 The Greek word translated as "fullness" means *repletion, completion, what fills,* and it is rooted in a word that means to *finish a period or task, to verify a prediction.* "Come in" means to *enter.* Thus we see that, having essentially completed his task of preaching the Gospel, YHVH now wants Ephraim to verify something to Judah by learning to honor the wisdom of Torah and celebrate Israel's feasts as never before! *Pleroma: Strong's #'s* G 4138 and 4137. Come in: *Strong's # G* 1525.
45 Thanks to Drs. Alex and Georgina Perdomo of Ocoee, FL for this insight and for their Power Point study of the matter.

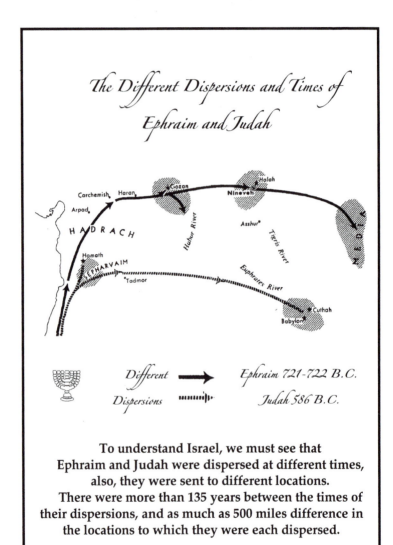

To understand Israel, we must see that
Ephraim and Judah were dispersed at different times,
also, they were sent to different locations.
There were more than 135 years between the times of
their dispersions, and as much as 500 miles difference in
the locations to which they were each dispersed.

Nine

Israel Revealed

The Gospels essentially tell the same story, but each Book serves a different purpose and adds new insights. Similarly, we now offer another review that will add new and different insights. Our hope is that this recap will help make these exciting truths even clearer. Like the previous chapter, this one too can be used in a group Bible study: Just read the outline statements, then the Scriptures references, and have a friendly, Spirit-led discussion.

The brief statements and following verse references reveal Israel's reemerging two houses, as well as the Father's latter-day plan for their full restoration. Study each verse referenced and ask the *Ruach HaKodesh* to keep you from all error and guide you into His truth.

For a thorough study of both of Israel's houses (Isaiah 8:14), we invite you to read the comprehensive books, *Redeemed Israel—Reunited and Restored* by Batya Wootten, and *Restoring Israel's Kingdom* by Angus Wootten. To celebrate Israel's feasts in light of her restoration, see the exciting Scripture-based book, *Israel's Feasts and their Fullness* (Batya Wootten, Key of David Publishing).

For more enlightening books about various aspects of Israel's restoration, see the Key of David Book Section.

• Abraham was promised that myriads of physical descendants would come from his own loins and be like the stars for number (Gen 12:3; 15:1-6; 17:1-6; Rom 4:19-22).

• Abraham and Sarah were promised myriads of biological heirs. This blessing of multiplicity of their seed was then given to their son, Isaac, and then to Jacob. The three patriarchs are called "joint heirs" (Gen 15:1-6; 26:3; 28:4; 1 Chr 16:16-17; Heb 11:9,39-40).

• Abraham's blessing was given to Isaac, to Jacob, to Joseph, and then Jacob gave it to Joseph's son, Ephraim (Gen 12:3; 15:5; 17:4; 26:4; 24:24,60; 28:3,14; 32:12; 48:4,16,19).

• Joseph was Jacob's chosen firstborn heir. When Jacob crossed his arms and chose and blessed Joseph's younger son, Ephraim, Jacob declared him to be Joseph's firstborn heir. Ephraim then became his Grandfather's primary heir, and thus the primary heir of Jacob/Israel (Gen 48:1-22; 1 Chr 5:1-2; Deu 21:17; Eze 37:19; Jer 31:9).

• Ephraim, his seed, and the heirs of the ten tribes of his Northern Kingdom were destined to become a *melo hagoyim*, a fullness of the Gentiles (Gen 48:19; Rom 11:25; Isa 8:14. To see *melo*/fullness used elsewhere see Psalm 24:1).

• Israel was divided into two houses, into Northern and Southern Kingdoms, which kingdoms were known as Israel (Ephraim) and Judah (1 Ki 11:11-13, 26,31-35; 12:15, 24; 2 Chr 11:4; Isa 8:14).

• In Israel, the firstborn heir was given two gifts: preeminence and a double portion—these giftings empowered him to be a *redeemer* to his brethren in times of trouble. This position is now in the hands of Ephraim's heirs (Deu 21:17 25:5-9; Exo 4:22; Jer 31:9; Ruth 3:9; Isa 59:20; 61:7; Gen 48:22; 1 Chr 5:1-2; Eze 37:18).

• The people of the Kingdom of Ephraim were sent into captivity into the territories of Assyria (around 722 BC). Judah was later sent to Babylon (around 586 BC). It is important to see that these were two very different captivities, and that there were many years and miles of difference in their dispersions (2 Ki 17:6,24; 1 Chr 5:26; Eze 1:1; 1 Ki 14:15).

• Ephraim became *"LoAmi"* (Not A People) and was *swallowed up* among the nations. They forgot the law of God, so He said He would, in turn, forget their children —but only for a season. They and their children thus became lost to their Israelite identity and heritage (Hos 1:10; 2:1,21-23; 4:1,6; 8:8; 11:9; Jer 31:20; Rom 9:23; Amos 9:9).

• The heirs of Israel were forever *chosen to choose*.[46] All Israelites and their seed must choose to either follow and obey the Holy One of Israel or to follow after false Gods (Deu 28:1-68; 30:19; Josh 24:15).

• The facts about our biological heritage cannot be changed due to faith or a lack thereof. What we do, or do not do, cannot change the facts about who are our actual physical forefathers. All Israelites are forever biological Israelites, and, there is an eternal call on their seed. Moreover, just as Judah and his heirs are part of the chosen people, so too are Ephraim's heirs part of Israel (Deu 4:37; 7:6-8; 10:15; Exo 19:4-6; Jer 31:37; 33:25-26; Rom 11:28-29).

• Although they were scattered among the nations, lost Ephraimites continue to be physical Israelites, just as Judahites continue to be physical Jews (Jer 31:20; 2 Ki 17:23; Zech 11:14; Dan 9:7; 1 Chr 5:26; Eph 2:17; Hosea 5:3; 8:8; Amos 9:9; Deu 28:64).

• Ephraim has been "lost" to, and is ignorant of, his own Israelite heritage. Because they rejected the eternal knowledge of YHVH's precepts, He in turn "forgot" their children. Yet, in His all-seeing eyes, they continued to be His "hidden ones," they continued to be a people who were

---

46 The *Theological Wordbook of the Old Testament* says of the Hebrew word, *bachar*, or *chosen*: "The root idea is evidently to 'take a keen look at'...thus...the connotation of 'testing or examining' found in Isaiah 48:10....The word is [primarily] used to express the *choosing* which has ultimate and eternal significance" (Moody Press, 1985, # 231, Vol. I, p 100).

destined for restoration in Messiah. The Father has always said of them, "I know Ephraim, and Israel is not hidden from Me" (Jer 31:18-19; Hos 1-2; 4:1,6; 5:3; Zec 10:6-9).

• Ezra spoke of a sacrifice that was made for "all Israel." Some say this action proves that *all biological Israelites* were present at the time. However, even as the Jewish people who remained in Babylon continued to be Jews, so the great majority of Ephraimites who were not present for the sacrifice continued to be lost and scattered heirs of Israel (Ezra 8:25; 1 Ki 12:20). The "all" in this verse speaks of *those present*. This same Hebrew word is used in a similar *limited* sense in 1 Samuel 18:16.

• The hallmarks of reunited Israel are: They will be sinless (blameless), not ever again uprooted from their Promised Land, and Messiah Yeshua will be their Lord and King (Isa 11:11-14; Jer 3:14-18; 16:11-16; 50:4-5,20; Zech 8:3,7,13; 9:13; 10:7-10; Hosea 11:10; Obad 1:18; 1 Sam 17:45; Eze 37:22-26; Isa 27:9).

• Ephraim and Judah are called Yah's two chosen families, nations, kingdoms, and houses (Jer 33:23-26; Eze 35:10; 37:22; Isa 8:14; Zech 2:12; 1 Pet 1:1; 2:9).

• The chosen people of Israel, both Judah and Ephraim, have been and are YHVH's two witnesses. While two individual "witnesses" may arise in the last days, the fact is that, historically, the two groups that are Christians and Jews are the only two groups on the face of the earth that have been witnesses for "the God of Abraham, Isaac, and Jacob" (Isa 43:8-13; 44:8; Num 35:30; Deu 17:6; 19:15; John 8:17; 10:35; Acts 3:13; 2 Cor 13:1).

• YHVH said, in Israel, matters must be confirmed by two or more witnesses. He calls Israel His witnesses and He divided them into two houses. In this way He has "two witness groups" who affirm His truths to the world (2 Chr 11:4; Isa 43:10; Num 13:2,6,8; 35:30; Deu 17:6; 19:15; John 8:17; 2 Cor 13:1; Rev 11:3,4; 1:20 Zech 4:11,14).

• Messiah Yeshua is also named Israel and He has been gathering the scattered seed of Jacob/Israel (Isa 49:1-6; 42:6-7; 9:2; Matt 1:18-,21; 2:15; 4:14-16; Rev 2:16; Eze 34:10; John 10:11; Luke 2:32).

• Yeshua made the New Covenant that was promised to both Israel and Judah with His Disciples. As heirs of Israel they were seated with Messiah Yeshua at His New Covenant Passover table and they drank of His covenant cup (Jer 31:31-33; Luke 22:20; Heb 8:6-12; 1 Cor 5:7).

• Yeshua is the Good Shepherd. He has one flock and is one with the Father. Together they have one people. However, earthly Israel can be in various stages of "acceptability" to Him. Restated, Israelites can be blessed or cursed and partake of some or all of her covenants (John 10:16,27-30; 17:11,20-21; Matt 2:6; 15:24; 1 John 5:8; Eze 34; Deu 28).

• Foreigners joined ancient Israel by observing circumcision, Passover, and sojourning. These three requirements were declared to be perpetual statutes in Israel. When fulfilled, the sojourner these requirementss was thereafter to be regarded as "a native of the Land" (Lev 19:34; Num 9:14; 15:15,16; Deu 18:15-19; Isa 56:3,6-8; Eze 47:23).

• These three citizenship rules were continued in New Covenant Israel. In Yeshua's Kingdom they are: **1)** circumcision of the heart; **2)** partaking of His Passover Bread and Wine; **3)** living in harmony with those of His Kingdom (Jer 4:4; 31:33; Dan 7:9-22; Mat 21:43; Luke 12:32; 22:30; John 1:29; Acts 1:6; 15:21; Eph 2:12-19; 1 Cor 5:7; Heb 7:12,27; 10:10; 1 Pet 1:1; 2:9; Rev 3:20).

• In the New Covenant, non-Jewish Believers are called *former* Gentiles. Once they come to faith in the Messiah they are no longer heathen Gentiles nor of foreign nations. They are called to walk as Israelites and be full members of His commonwealth. They are being ruled by the God of Israel and are part of His chosen people (Matt 18:17; 5:47; 6:7; 2 Cor 6:17; Eph 2:11-22; 1 Thes 4:5; 1 Pet 2:12).

- The *church/ekklesia/congregation* of Israel was in the wilderness and was thought to be one with Israel. It is not "separate from Israel" as is often taught (Acts 7:38; Heb 4:2).
- Believers belong to Messiah Yeshua's *ekklesia*, to His *"congregation* of the firstborn." The Father Himself calls Ephraim His "firstborn" (Jer 31:9; Heb 12:22-23).
- Ephraim is not the only son who needs to be adopted. The word *adoption* is used only five times in Scripture. The five verses do not speak of us becoming sons of Abraham but "sons of God." All who would be His eternal sons, Jew and non-Jew alike, must receive this spirit of adoption. Moreover, it is specifically said to "belong to the sons of Israel." When we are born from above we become adopted sons of God and thus have the promise of eternal life in Messiah (Rom 8:15,16,23; 9:4; Gal 4:5; Eph 1:5).
- YHVH wants us to worship Him in spirit and truth. All Israelites are called to be spiritual, and all spiritual people are physical. When we are reborn from above we become sons of the God of Israel. Our actual physical heritage is an unknown factor. Abraham was promised myriads of physical heirs and many of Messiah's followers probably are actual sons of Abraham, yet a genetic connection cannot be absolutely proven. This caveat is true for Jew and non-Jew alike (John 4:23; Gen 12:3; 15:1-6; 17:1-6).
- Israel's olive tree had two major branches, Ephraim and Judah. Its Root, or Life-source, is the Messiah. Even the patriarchs looked to Him as their Life-Source (Jer 11:10,16; 2:18,21; Rom 11:25; Isa 8:13-14; Rev 22:16; Rom 3:23).
- Believers in the Messiah are not to be arrogant toward the Jewish branches that were broken off for unbelief. Instead, they are to lovingly provoke Judah to jealousy, that he might be regrafted back into Messiah's Olive Tree (Obad 1:12; Joel 2:32-3:1; Luke 13:1-5; Rom 11:11,18-21).
- Like the parable of the prodigal son, there is an ancient sibling rivalry between Ephraim and Judah. As

Ephraim emerges from his 2730 years of captivity,[47] he is jealous of Judah and his roots. In turn, Judah vexes Ephraim by refusing to recognize him as an equal heir in Israel. To end their ancient quarrel Ephraim needs to change first and thus cause Judah to see something in him that he wants (Isa 11:13; Jer 31:18,19).

• Ephraim will repent of his youthful sins when he is instructed about his own Israelite roots, when he comes to know himself and understands that he, too, is part of Israel. He also needs to realize that Judah is his brother and he must begin to treat him as such (Jer 31:18,19).

• Ephraim was called to be a watchman for the whole house of Israel (Hosea 9:8; Jer 31:6; 30:24; Isa 48:6; Hab 2:1). He is especially called to guard the people, to warn of impending danger, to care for those who are in trouble.[48]

• Ephraim is destined to return to the Promised Land in righteousness, in might, and in the power of the Holy Spirit. He is meant to re-examine the truth about the Ruach HaKodesh and the restoration of the whole house of Israel (Jer 31:21; Eze 37:23; Hosea 1:10; Zec 10:7).[49]

• The first example in Scripture of two witnesses who gave a good report about the abilities of the God of Israel were the two spies, Joshua and Caleb. They are the first "two witnesses" and they were from the tribes of Ephraim and Judah (Num 13:2,6,8).

• Yeshua gives His two witnesses the power to prophesy and He describes them as two olive trees and two lampstands. Lampstands also are called *ekklesias*/congregations. In the last days, YHVH calls forth two congregations of peoples. There could also be two individual witnesses who arise in the last days, and it is possible that they might lead the two reunited houses of Israel in a war against the Beast (Rev 1:20; 11:3,4; 16:3-4,11-20).

---

47 See "Ephraim's Punishment" Chart, page 26.
48 *Shamar: S&BDB* # H 8104; *Tsaphah:* # 6822; Watch: # H 4931.
49 See the books, *The Voice... Hearing the Almighty* by Batya Wootten. And, *Israel—Empowered by The Spirit* by Wallace E. Smith and Batya Wootten .

- Zechariah said two olive trees are anointed to serve the LORD of all the earth. He is calling to two congregations of people—Judah and Ephraim. He is making their two sticks (trees) one in His hand. Books are made from trees and the two Books of Old and New Covenants need to be affirmed by the two witnesses, Judah and Ephraim. We need to learn to see the Old and New Covenants as one Book of Covenants (Eze 37:15-28; Zec 4:11,14).

- Our Father long-ago declared His latter-day plan to reunite both the houses of Israel: A remnant from both houses will come to true repentance and be rejoined to one another in the power of the Ruach haKodesh (Deu 33:7; Isa 27:9; Jer 3:17-18; 50:4; Dan 7:27; Hosea 11:8-10; Amos 9:11; Zech 4:6; 8:23; Micah 5:3; Luke 12:32; Rom 11).

- Judah will believe in Messiah when he sees Ephraim, especially as part of reunited Israel, properly representing both the Messiah and the Torah. Judah has been blind to the Messiah and Ephraim has been blind to the truths of Torah. Now is the time for both houses to begin to see the full truth of Scripture. We need to work to help make these truths known (Mat 23:37-39; Rom 11; Isa 8:14).

- When Ephraim and Judah are united in YHVH Elohim, when their reunion is fully manifested, when they become like their Messiah, loving not their lives even unto death, then they will become a sinless, blameless, invincible army. When they are ready to lay down their lives for their faith, then they will be sovereignly empowered to fight the battles of the God of Israel (Isa 11:14; Hosea 1:11; Amos 9:10; Zech 9:13- 10:10; 13:2; Zeph 3:11-13).

- *Shema Yisrael... Hear and obey O Israel* (Gen 49:2; Deu 6:4; Eze 36:1; Hosea 5:1).

Ten

There Are Two...

Y HVH is dealing with *two* houses of Israel. He has:

- **Two** Houses (Isa 8:14; Jer 31:31-33; Heb 8:8-10)
- **Two** Nations (Eze 35:10)
- **Two** Chosen Families (Jer 33:24)
- **Two** Sisters (Eze 23:2-4)
- **Two** Olive Branches (Zech 4:11-14; Jer 11:10, 16-17; 2:18,21; Rom 11; Rev 11:4)
- **Two** Sticks (Eze 37:15-28)
- **Two** Witnesses (Rev 11:3-4)
- **Two** Lampstands (Rev 11:3-4)
- **Two** Silver Trumpets (Num 10:2-3)
- **Two** Leavened Loaves (Heb 9:28)
- **Two** Cherubim (Exo 25:18-20)
- **Two** Armies That Dance (Song of Songs 6:4,13)

To understand Israel, we must realize that the Father has been dealing with *two* houses of Israel, Judah and Ephraim, and He now wants us to become *one* stick in His hand (Eze 37:15-28).[50]

---

50 Using the above list, Kelly Ferrari has written a song titled, "Two by Two." It is from her album, titled, "Covenant With Israel," © Kelly Ferrari and Mama Rose Music (606041299429). See it at: http://www.doorkeeperministries.com

We need to become one because our God is One and His people are called to be one. Ephraim and Judah have served their individual purposes in establishing the two immutable truths of Law and salvation by Grace. But now it is time for them to grow beyond that which they have understood about these truths in the past. It is time for both to leave behind their errors and join together, brother with brother. Then, and only then, will we see the power of our God moving in the earth on a level that rivals the experiences of our forefathers. Then we will begin to see His mighty hand of deliverance in our day...

Father, we ask You to pour out Your Ruach HaKodesh on us, to enlighten the eyes of our heart that we might see the hope to which You have called us. Allow us to get a glimpse the riches and glorious inheritance You have in store for us. Help us to come to know, and fully trust in, Your incredible power. Give us a vision of greatness of Your call to us in Messiah Yeshua. Help us to know that You dwell far above all rule and authority and power and dominion, that Your Name is above every name that is named, and that You have placed Your Glorious Name on us.[51]

We ask You to fill us, to lead, guide, protect, and empower us. Allow us to be used in this day to help proclaim Messiah Yeshua's Gospel of the Kingdom. In His Name we pray.

Amen and Amen.

---

[51] Num 6:27; Eph 1:13; 4:30; Rev 7:3-4.

Addendum A

Key Verses to Remember

To help us understand and share our faith about both houses of Israel we can cross-reference some affirming Scriptures in our Bibles. For example, next to Genesis 48:19, write in Psalm 24:1 and Romans 11:25. At Romans 11:25 write in Genesis 48:19 and Psalm 24:1, and so on. In this way, if we remember only one of the verses related to the subject, we can pick up the trail that leads to the other confirming verses.

Here we offer brief overview statements followed by the particular verses that relate to the statements.

Ephraim: A *Melo haGoyim:*

Ephraim was destined to become a "fullness [*melo*] of Gentiles." Psalm 24:1 also uses "fullness [*melo*]" and thus helps us define the word, which speaks of vast numbers of biological heirs from Ephraim's tribes. Romans Eleven explains that a partial hardening happened to Israel (both houses) and that this hardening, this inability to see, was to last until "the fullness of Gentiles" was come in. In other words, *we could not see the fullness of this truth until now, until this particular point in time!*

Jacob "refused and said, 'I know, my son...he [Manasseh] also will become a people and he also will be great. However, his younger brother shall be greater than he, and his descendants shall become a [*melo hagoyim*] fullness of the nations'" (Genesis 48:19).

"The earth is YHVH's, and the [*melo*] fullness thereof" (Psalm24:1, KJV).

"For I do not want you, brethren, to be uninformed of this mystery—so that you will not be wise [conceited] in your own estimation—that a partial hardening has happened to Israel until the fullness of the Gentiles has come in" (Romans 11:25).

Two Stumbling Houses of Israel

Both the houses of Israel were destined to stumble over the Sanctuary, Who is Messiah Yeshua. This in turn means that *after* the time of Yeshua, there still had to be two separate houses of Israel that would stumble over Him. They would stumble because both houses were part of Israel's Twelve Tribes, and *all of Israel* was hardened and blinded, although in different ways.

John reveals that the "Temple/Sanctuary" is Yeshua. He also says that when Messiah Yeshua rose from the dead, His disciples "believed the Scripture." This is a reference to Isaiah 8:13-14. They are the only verses that speak of the Holy One becoming a Sanctuary over which Israel would stumble.

In Romans 11 we see that Israel stumbled because they were hardened, or blinded to the truth.

Affirming Scriptures:

"...YHVH of hosts...shall become a sanctuary; but to both the houses of Israel, a stone to strike and a rock to stumble over..." (Isaiah 8:13-14).

Yeshua said, "Destroy this temple, and in three days I will raise it up.' The Jews then said, 'It took forty-six years to build this temple, and will You raise it up in three days?'

But He was speaking of the temple [sanctuary] of His body. When He was raised from the dead, His disciples remembered that He said this; and they believed the Scripture and the word which Yeshua had spoken" (John 2:19-22).

"For I do not want you, brethren, to be uninformed of this mystery—so that you will not be wise in your own estimation—that a partial hardening has happened to Israel [both houses] until the fullness of the Gentiles [see Genesis 48:19] has come in" (Romans 11:25).

The Patriarchs and Myriads of Heirs

Abraham, Isaac, and Jacob were promised myriads of physical descendants. The essence of this blessing of multiplicity was passed to Joseph's son, Ephraim. If we have the "faith of Abraham," we too will believe that myriads of descendants sprang from his loins, and that they were to become a "great congregation of peoples." This is not to say that all Believers *must* be physical heirs, but to emphasize that myriads of physical heirs were promised to Abraham. Only the Father in Heaven knows their actual number, and, no one can absolutely prove that we *are*, or *are not*, biological descendants of Abraham.

Many non-Jewish Believers have been told that they are not part of Israel and the end result is that a great number of them have denied their faith in Jesus Christ and converted to Judaism—so they can "belong to Israel."

Affirming Scriptures:
"After these things the word of the LORD came to Abram in a vision, saying, 'Do not fear, Abram, I am a shield to you; Your reward shall be very great.' Abram said, 'O Lord God, what will You give me, since I am childless, and the heir of my house is Eliezer of Damascus?' And Abram said, 'Since You have given no offspring to me, one born in my house is my heir.' Then behold, the word of the LORD came to him, saying, 'This man will not be your heir; but one

who will come forth from your own body, he shall be your heir.' And He took him outside and said, 'Now look toward the heavens, and count the stars, if you are able to count them.' And He said to him, 'So shall your descendants be.' Then he believed in the LORD; and He reckoned it to him as righteousness" (Genesis 15:1-6).

YHVH also said, "'I am the Almighty God, walk before Me and be blameless. And I will establish My covenant between Me and you, and I will multiply you exceedingly.' And Abram fell on his face, and God talked with him, saying, 'Behold, My covenant is with you, and you will be the father of a multitude of nations. No longer shall your name be called Abram, or "exalted father," but your name shall be Abraham, "father of a multitude." For I will make you the father of a multitude of nations.[52] I will make you exceedingly fruitful, I will make nations of you'" (Genesis 17:1-6).

The New Covenant says, "Without becoming weak in faith he contemplated his own body, now as good as dead since he was about a hundred years old, and the deadness of Sarah's womb; yet, with respect to the promise of God, he did not waver in unbelief, but grew strong in faith, giving glory to God, and being fully assured that what He had promised, He was able also to perform. Therefore, 'It was reckoned to him as righteousness'" (Romans 4:19-22).

YHVH promised to make the "fewest of all peoples... as numerous as the stars of the sky" (Deuteronomy 7:7; Exodus 32:13). The miracle of His promise to Abraham is that the *few* become *many*. We see that "many" when we include Ephraim in our "Israel picture." Thus Paul writes, "If you belong to Messiah, then you are Abraham's descendants, heirs according to promise (Galatians 3:29).

---

52 Abraham believed he would father a multitude of nations, *hamon goyim* (גוים המון). *Strong's* says *Goyim* (גוים), the Hebrew word for Gentiles/Nations (# H1471) means, a foreign nation, heathen people. *The New Brown-Driver-Briggs-Gesenius Hebrew-Aramaic Lexicon* says *goyim* means nation, people, and it usually speaks of non-Hebrews (#H1471; Hendrickson, 1979; Parsons Technology, 1999). The *Theological Wordbook of the Old Testament* 2 Vol., Moody, 1981, says, "goyim... usually refers to..the surrounding pagan nations" (# 326e).

YHVH promised Isaac, "I will multiply[53] your descendants as the stars of heaven" (Genesis 26:4).

The blessing that was given Isaac's wife, Rebekah, was, "Be the mother of thousands of millions," or, "myriads" (Genesis 24:60).[54]

Together, they passed their multitudinous blessing to their son Jacob: "May God...make you fruitful and multiply you, that you may become a congregation of peoples"[55] (Genesis 28:3).

The Father promised Jacob/Israel, "Thy seed shall be as the dust of the earth, and thou shalt spread abroad to the west, and to the east, and to the north, and to the south" (Genesis 28:14, KJV).

Jacob said Joseph's son, Ephraim, would become a "fullness of Gentile Nations" (Genesis 48:19).

Separating the Patriarchal Blessings Taking the Ekklesia Out of Israel

Some people try to separate the blessing of Abraham from that of Isaac and Jacob claiming that non-Jews are "spiritual heirs" of Abraham, but are not physical heirs of Isaac and Jacob. However, Abraham's blessing cannot be separated from that of Isaac and Jacob, because the three were joint heirs.[56] In addition, many mistakenly try to separate the true *ekklesia* (church) from Biblical Israel. Yet neither of these positions are Scriptural concepts.

---

53 Multiply, *rabah* (רבה), means to increase, exceedingly, become numerous, great. See *S&BDB* # H 7235; *TWOT* # 2103, 2104.

54 *S&BDB* #'s H 505 and 7235.

55 From Jacob YHVH would call forth a *congregation*—a *kahal* (קהל). This Hebrew word is primarily translated *congregation* and is especially used to describe an assembly, company, congregation, or convocation, called together by the Almighty for religious purposes. See *TWOT* # 1991a; also *S&BDB* # H 6951.

56 Abraham and Sarah were promised a son, Isaac. Abraham instead had a child with Sarah's handmaiden, Hagar, who gave birth to Ishmael, who was to become 12 nations. However, the promise was to Abraham and Sarah. Isaac was thus given the promise of Abraham (Gen 17:15-22; 18:10-14; Rom 4:19-22; 9:9).

Affirming Scriptures:

YHVH said to Isaac, "To you and to your seed...I will establish the oath which I swore to your father Abraham" (Genesis 26:3).

Isaac said to Jacob, "May He [YHVH] also give you the blessing of Abraham" (Genesis 28:4).

"The covenant which ... [God] made with Abraham, and His oath to Isaac, He also confirmed to Jacob for a statute, to Israel as an everlasting covenant" (1 Chronicles 16:16-17).

Abraham "lived as an alien in the land of promise ... with Isaac and Jacob, fellow heirs of the same promise" (Hebrews 11:9).

"These [Patriarch] were all commended for their faith, yet none of them received what had been promised... only together with us [the New Covenant Believers[57]] would they be made perfect" (Hebrews 11:39-40, NIV).

In the *Brit Chadashah* (New Covenant), ancient Israel is called "the *ekklesia* [congregation] that was in the wilderness" (Acts 7:38).

Messiah Yeshua used *ekklesia*, the word usually translated (or mistranslated) "church,"[58] to speak of the assembly He was *building*, or *rebuilding*—even as He had promised (Jeremiah 31:4; 33:6-7; Matthew 16:18; 18:17).

---

57 "The prophets... made careful search and inquiry, seeking to know what person or time the Spirit... was indicating.... It was revealed... that they were not serving themselves, but you, in these things which now have been announced to you through those who preached the gospel by the Holy Spirit" (1 Pet 1:10-12).
58 "Church," like "Israel," is a multi-faceted name/title, and one must know what is meant with its use: i.e., there is a "church system" that persecutes true Believers (Rev 3:16; 2 Tim 3:1-12; Matt 5:20), and a true *church*, an eternal *ekklesia*—which includes all who truly seek to follow the God of Israel (Acts 7:38; 2 Thes 1:1; 2:13). There is also a "Synagogue of Satan" that opposes Yeshua (John 8:44; 10:33; Rev 2:9; 3:9). In this work, the word "church" is sometimes used to include those who, in this life claim to belong to "the church." This standard of including those who, in the end, the Father Himself may not include, also is applied in references to Jews and Judaism. We trust that in the end, the Holy One Himself will decide who among both peoples is acceptable (Mat 7:23). The word "church" is often misunderstood so we prefer the Greek *ekklesia* (*Strong's* # G 1577) when referring to the *called out ones*. As stated above, Messiah is "rebuilding" His *ekklesia* of Israel.

We conclude that both Yeshua and the First Century Believers knew that Israel, the *kahal*[59] and *ekklesia*,[60] were one and the same. Just as our God is One, so in the end He will have but one called-out people.[61]

Adoption and Israel's Sons

Many people believe that only the non-Jewish Believers in Messiah have to be adopted. However, *all* Believers must receive the "spirit of adoption." When they do, they become "sons of God." Receiving this adoption empowers us to call the Almighty our Abba (Father). The fullness of our adoption is expressed in the redemption of our bodies. This spirit of adoption is specifically said to "belong to the sons of Israel." It likewise was given to the "saints" at Ephesus. The spirit of adoption is mentioned only five times in Scripture, and the verses do not even mention Abraham. They do not speak of non-Jewish Believers being adopted into Abraham's family. They instead speak of us becoming "born-again" sons of the Holy One.

Affirming Scriptures:

Paul tells those being led by the Spirit of God, "You have not received a spirit of slavery leading to fear again, but you have received a spirit of adoption as sons by which we cry out, "Abba! Father!" (Romans 8:15).

---

59 According to the *Theological Wordbook...*, "Usually *kahal* is translated *ekklesia* in the LXX [*Septuagint*]." See *TWOT* word # 1991a; page 790. *Septuagint*: Greek translation of the Hebrew Old Covenant completed 200 years before Messiah's birth. Of the 122 KJV usages, more than 60 times *kahal* (*kehilat*) is translated *ekklesia* (*Hatch and Redpath Concordance to the Septuagint*, 1983, Baker, p 433); 36 times it is translated *synagogue*, as in Genesis 28:3 (*TWOT* word # 1991a). Like *ekklesia, kahal* and synagogue also describe an *assembly* (Strong's #'s H6951; G4864).

60 *Ekklesia* (εκκλησια), the New Covenant word translated *church* speaks of a "calling out," of a *meeting*, especially a religious *congregation*, an assembly (*Thayer's Greek-English Lexicon of the New Testament*, Baker, 1983, p 196a; *Strong's* # G 1577). In Acts 19:32 *ekklesia* is used to define the confused mob crying out against Paul. Thus, *assembly* might be a more appropriate translation.

61 One God: Deu 6:4; Mark 12:29. One people: Num 15:15; Eze 37:19; John 17:11.

"The Spirit Himself testifies with our spirit that we are children of God....And...we ourselves, having the first fruits of the Spirit, even we ourselves groan within ourselves, waiting eagerly for our adoption as sons, the redemption of our body" (Romans 8:16,23).

Paul spoke of his kinsmen according to the flesh and he said they "are Israelites, to whom belongs the adoption as sons, and the glory and the covenants and the giving of the Law and the temple service and the promises" (Romans 9:4).

Paul also says YHVH wanted to "redeem those who were under the Law, that we might receive the adoption as sons" (Galatians 4:5). He also wrote to the saints at Ephesus and told them that, YHVH "predestined us to adoption as sons through Messiah Yeshua to Himself, according to the kind intention of His will" (Ephesians 1:5).

The Olive Tree of Israel

Israel was first called an olive tree when Jeremiah spoke to "the house of Israel and the house of Judah." Thus, we see two main branches in this tree. The first branches to be broken off were those of Israel (Ephraim). YHVH then scattered Ephraim among every nation, and there, they became degenerate and wild. Branches from Judah were later broken off when they were scattered to Babylon. Seventy years later, some from Judah returned to the Land (around Daniel's time), however, most of Judah continued to be broken off the tree and remained behind in Babylon. The tree was thus partially denuded at the times of Messiah and Paul.

Yeshua is the Root of Israel's olive tree, meaning, He is its *life-source*. Even the patriarchs must have faith in and receive eternal life from Him.

(See the two Olive Tree Diagrams: "The Two Branches in The Olive Tree," page ix, and, the "Five Stages of Israel's Olive Tree," page x).

Addendum A: Key Verses to Remember

Affirming Scriptures:

When YHVH called Israel an olive tree, Jeremiah spoke of both Israel (Ephraim) and Judah, and said, "YHVH called your name, 'A green olive tree, beautiful in fruit and form'" (Jeremiah 11:16).

"Israel [Ephraim] is swallowed up; they are now among the nations like a vessel in which no one delights" (Hosea 8:8; also see Romans 9:21-24).

"I will shake the house of Israel among all nations as grain is shaken in a sieve, but not a kernel will fall to the ground [meaning, *be lost to Me*]" (Amos 9:9; see Hosea 5:3).

YHVH asked of Ephraim (who was taken captive to Assyria), "What are you doing...on the road to Assyria?" He also said, "I planted you a choice vine, a completely faithful seed. How then have you turned yourself before Me into the degenerate shoots of a foreign vine?" (Jeremiah 2:18,21). (For all outward purposes "lost" Ephraim became like degenerate foreigners, like the heathen of the nations.)

YHVH said, both "the house of Israel and the house of Judah have broken My covenant, which I made with their fathers." And that, both "Israel and...Judah...provoke Me by offering sacrifices to Baal" (Jeremiah 11:10, 17).

King David said he was like a green olive tree, and that his children/seed were like olive plants. Messiah Yeshua is the greater Son of David, and He said of Himself, "I am the root and offspring/descendant of David, the bright and morning star" (Psalm 52:8; 128:3; Revelation 22:16).

When the apostle Paul spoke of wild olive branches being "grafted into...the rich root of the olive tree," he was referring to those of the olive tree that YHVH had largely denuded by the time Ephraim was scattered among the nations and Judah sent to Babylon (Romans 11:17).

Some of Judah returned from Babylon and were in the Land at the time of Messiah (Ezra 2:1; Daniel 9:25-26).

Concerning this partial return, Paul said, some of Judah's branches "were broken off...for their unbelief." Those of Judah who rejected Yeshua as Messiah were then broken off of His tree and need to be grafted in again.

Those who believed in Him remained in His olive tree because they acknowledged Him as being their Life-source (Romans 11:17-24).

So, what is the "mystery" of which Paul spoke?

The mystery is about the re-gathering of Ephraim—and about he and his companions changing in such a way that they are empowered to provoke Judah to jealousy, to make Judah want to once more be part of Messiah's olive tree!

Ephraim and Judah have both been in stages of being natural and wild branches. We see this in that both have been close to the Cultivator—and being close to Him is what keeps this tree in its *natural, cultivated* state.[62]

Messiah Yeshua said, "I am the true vine, and My Father is the vinedresser. Every branch in Me that does not bear fruit, He takes away; and every branch that bears fruit, He prunes it so that it may bear more fruit" (John 15:1).

Finally, we see that *both* groups, natural and wild, are called *olive branches*. Since Israel is the olive tree we conclude that both groups—*and their respective companions* —each represent a part, but not the whole, of Israel (Jeremiah 11:10,16; Romans 11:17,25; Ezekiel 37 :16-17).

---

[62] Although Scripture calls Judah "natural" branches, Paul is principally addressing their *natural disposition*, and not their *biological descent* (See *Strong's #*'s G 5449, 2798). Also see the book, *Redeemed Israel*, chapters 14-15, and 21.

Addendum B

Prayer Points

Ephraim was especially called to be a "watchman" for the whole house of Israel. He is called to cry out, "O YHVH, save Thy people the remnant of Israel" (Psalm 5:3; Jeremiah 31:7; 30:24; Hosea 9:8).

We need watchmen who know that "the effective, fervent prayer of a righteous man availeth much" (James 5:16, KJV): *Effective*: he sees the problem. *Fervent*: he cares about solving it. *Righteous*: he is covered by Messiah's blood. Those who see the truth about "both the houses of Israel" need to pray for her full restoration.

Between the feasts of Yom Teruah and Yom Kippur lie ten days that are traditionally known as "The Ten Days of Awe." It is thought to be a time when brother should especially seek to make peace with brother, before the judgment that comes with the great and awesome day of Yom Kippur. These days teach us the importance of making peace with our brothers before Messiah's return.

The following Prayer Points and Yom Teruah feast explanations are reproduced from the book, *Israel's Feasts and their Fullness*, chapter 29, "Ten Days of Prayer."

While the prayers were especially written for the Ten Days of Awe, they and the ideas about Yom Teruah are worth reviewing and praying at any time of the year.

Who is Israel? Redeemed Israel- *A Primer*

Begin Book Quote:

On the first day of the seventh month, Israel was to have a reminder, a blowing of trumpets (Lev 23:24).

Trumpets played an important role in ancient Israel's Tabernacle and Temple celebrations; 120 of them were sounded at the dedication of Solomon's Temple (2 Chr 5).

So how can we honor the feast of Yom Teruah in our day? [Some call this day *Rosh HaShanah*.]

When the people of Ezra's time celebrated this feast, Ezra read the Torah before the public assembly. Having the Father's law written on our hearts by His Spirit is the very heart of His New Covenant promise to us. We need to reread that law at this time in history. We need to hear the Father's Torah commands with the ears of the Spirit. Like our forefathers, we too need to return, we need to weep and come to a place of true repentance and restoration (Neh 7:73-8:2; Jer 15:19-21; 31:31-33; Heb 8:8-10).

We can honor this prophetic feast by beginning with a reading aloud of Numbers 10:1-10. If possible, have representatives of both Judah and Ephraim blow two silver trumpets in unison. Then, with a clarion call have them loudly proclaim: *"Let the twin voices of Ephraim and Judah be heard in this place!"*

To celebrate in this way is a stirring sight to behold. Something very precious in the spirit takes place when both the houses of Israel are properly honored, and when they speak in unison.

Reasonably priced silver plated trumpets are available on the Internet.[63] If you cannot afford them, go to a store that specializes in arts and crafts and purchase an inexpensive pair of brass plated trumpets and paint them with silver spray paint.

---

63 See www.messianicisrael.com. Note: These trumpets have rings for banners. Beautiful silk banners (including custom made banners and flags), can be found at www.jesuspaintings.com

Addendum B: Prayer Points

At your celebration, after having Judah and Ephraim enter with their trumpets, have two people dressed in white read aloud Psalms 93-100. These Psalms are believed to have been composed especially for the feast of Trumpets.[64]

In Jewish tradition, Psalm 47 is read aloud seven times:

> "O clap your hands, all ye people; shout unto God with the voice of triumph. For the LORD Most High is terrible; he is a great King over all the earth. He shall subdue the people under us, and the nations under our feet. He shall choose our inheritance for us, the excellency of Jacob whom he loved. *Selah*. God is gone up with a shout, the LORD with the sound of a trumpet. Sing praises to God, sing praises: sing praises unto our King, sing praises" (Psa 47:1-6).

Warring for Our Inheritance

It is important that we sound our united voices in prayer for all Israel during this time. We need to pray as Messiah's Body because reunited Israel is to sound the war alarm against enemies who come against the eternal plans of the Holy One (Isa 11:13-14). To do this, we first realize that, just as our forefathers were in bondage in Egypt, so we too are in bondage. Like them, we will be freed when we have a deep desire for deliverance.

When the king of Egypt died, the sons of Israel *cried out*. And, "their cry for help because of their bondage rose up to the LORD." He *heard their groaning*, then remembered His covenant with their fathers and took notice of them and their plight (Exo 2:23-25).

Crying out is key. Sincerely calling on the Holy One in true repentance will cause Him to take notice and deliver us! He said He would be like a lion to Ephraim and Judah.

---

64 See the book, *His Glory Revealed*, John Hagee, Nashville: Thomas Nelson Publishers, 1999, p 106.

He would tear to pieces and return to His place *until* we acknowledge our guilt and seek His face.

We first must admit to our sin, then *cry out* for deliverance from the Egypt that binds us. Like Daniel, we accept the fact that we have sinned and we repent, then Abba will take notice and redeem us. We first humble ourselves, then honor Him; we sincerely ask for pardon, praise Him, then humbly pray for deliverance from our situation (see Hos 5:14-15; 9:5-15; Mat 6:5-18).

Ten Days of Prayer

As we seek the Father's reunion plan for both the houses of Israel (Isa 11:13), we might want to sincerely pray the following suggested prayers during this time.[65]

- **Day 1**: Pray that all Israel might come to true repentance, that they might be saved. Pray that they would put away all of their idols and be granted a new heart and a new spirit, that they might live and not die (Isa 30:15; Eze 18:31-32). Pray that salvation in Yeshua will come to all Israel (Gen 48:19; Rom 11:25,26; Eph 4:15; Mat 1:21). Pray that the veil will be lifted from the eyes of both the houses of Israel so they will see the truth of Yeshua and cease to stumble over Him (Isa 8:14; Rom 11:25; John 2:22). Pray that as the Standard, Yeshua might be lifted up in all His glory, and that the world may see Him in truth, and not according to manmade religion (Isa 11:12).

- **Day 2**: Pray that all Israel will see the truth about the *melo hagoyim* promised to Ephraim, and that the fullness of Gentiles will come into their fullness, or

---

65 A "Ten Days of Prayer" pamphlet that can be carried in your Bible is available. See the Key of David Publishing section.

maturity. Pray that Ephraim will cease to be jealous of Judah, whether that jealousy is acted out in violence or in wishing they were Jewish. Pray that Ephraim will make Judah jealous rather than being jealous of Judah, which causes Ephraim to lose his effectiveness (Rom 9:25,26; 10:19; 11:11; Hos 1:9,0; 2:23). Pray that Ephraim will learn to judge with righteous judgment, and that in their desire to be reunited with Judah they will not trade errant Christian ways for errant Jewish ways (Isa 11:13; Jer 15:19-21; 31:21-25; John 7:24).

Day 3: Pray that all whom the Father has chosen to instruct Ephraim in this time will arise, and that Ephraim will come to repentance and be ashamed for the deeds of her youth (Jer 31:18-19). Pray that she will cease to be like a silly dove without sense and move beyond the elementary things and, press on to maturity (Hos 7:11; Heb 6:1-17). Pray that Ephraim repents of following man's commands and instead accepts Messiah's yoke of Torah (Hos 4:6; 5:11-6:3). Pray that Ephraim will fulfill her divine mandate, which is to walk in a way that honors Torah and thus provokes Judah to want what she has (Rom 11).

Day 4: Pray that the sheep would be delivered from wicked shepherds who muddy the waters and feed themselves rather than the flock. Pray that the sheep be snatched out of the hands of shepherds who divide Israel's flock. Pray that all wolves in sheep's clothing and all false prophets be exposed for who they are in truth (Deu 13:1-5; Eze 34; Jer 23:1-3; Mat 7:15). Pray that the spirit of Jezebel be rooted out from among us, that we would not lie or try to steal the field of others, and that Israel's prophets would not fear her. Pray that the spirit of Elijah might instead be fully released in our day. Pray that the hearts of the fathers might be turned to their children and the hearts of the children to their fathers. Pray for godly families to be raised up in both the houses of Israel (1 Ki 21: Hos 1:4-5; 2:22; Rev 2:20-22; Mal 4:5-6).

- **Day 5:** Pray for the safety and well-being of those of Judah who have returned to the Promised Land; pray their hearts will be turned toward their fathers and that angels will be given charge over them (Isa 11:11; Luke 1:17; Psa 91:11). Pray that even as the Father has gathered for a second time the dispersed of Judah, He will restore their fortunes. Pray that the Father possess Judah as His portion in the holy land, and again choose Jerusalem. Pray that He enter into judgment with those who harass Judah and Jerusalem. Pray that Judah might be healed of the hurts she experienced in her dispersion (Isa 11:11-13; Joel 3:1-2; Zec 2:12).

- **Day 6:** Pray that the Father will use the tragic events of our time to bring His people to repentance and faith in Him through the shed blood of Messiah Yeshua (Obad 1:12; Jer 5:12-14; Luke 13:1-5). Pray that wisdom and discernment will be granted to those who have influence over the nation of Israel in spiritual, political, and financial arenas (Dan 2:21; 4:32; 5:21; Rom 13:1). Pray that they realize that Ephraim is their brother, and that the only true answers are found in the true Gospel, in the sacrificial Lamb, and in He who paid the price for our sins that we might have eternal life in Him (1 Cor 7:23; Mat 27:9).

- **Day 7**: Pray that the hearts of Ephraim and Judah might be circumcised with a love for each other. Pray that each will learn to give credit where it is due, and that each will learn to objectively see the role they have played as part of the people of Israel: Ephraim in declaring salvation through Messiah, who is the Living Torah; and Judah in declaring the feasts and the eternal truths of the written Torah (Gen 48:19; Acts 1:8; Rom 4:15; 2 Chr 11:4; Eze 37:15-28).

- **Day 8**: Pray for both houses to see the Father's plan to have a pure, overcoming army, and to give themselves to becoming that army (Isa 11:11-14; 27:6-9; Zech 8:3,7,13; 9:13; 10:7-10; Hos 11:10; Obad 1:18; Jer 50:4,5,20; 3:14-18; Eze 37:22-26). Pray the sons of Israel come, they and the sons of Judah, and go along weeping in a true search for their God; pray they turn their faces toward Zion and truly be joined in covenant with Him (Jer 50:4-5; Hos 5:14-15). Pray that Ephraim would again be like a mighty man, with their heart glad as if from wine, and that their children see it and be glad and their heart rejoice in the LORD (Zec 10:7). Pray that all Israel will seek to pay the full price for their pardon, that all their pagan practices and idols will be made like chalk stones and unable to stand (Isa 27:9). Pray that Israel's mighty ones will be equipped with the breath of the Spirit of the Most High (Eze 37:10).

- **Day 9**: Pray for the peace of Jerusalem, and that they who love her would prosper, pray that peace would be within her walls and prosperity within her palaces (Psa 122:6,7). Pray for Jerusalem to become the City of Truth, and to acknowledge Messiah Yeshua as her King of Kings. Pray for

Believers to understand that Jerusalem is also a bride, and that she will come down from Heaven and her sons will then marry her. Pray for Believers to rise up and truly become her appointed watchmen (Psa 48:2; Isa 62:1-7; Zec 8:3; Mat 5:35; 23:37-39; Rev 17:14; 19:7,16; 21:2,9; 22:17).

- **Day 10**: Pray that the sons of Israel who are pursuing this work of restoration for the Kingdom would be strong and courageous. Pray that the spirit of Joshua and Caleb would be upon them, and that they would know that in the strength of the Holy One they can possess the Land (Josh 1:6-9,18; 10:25). Pray they would be given wisdom, discernment of spirits, and a double portion of the Holy Spirit as they seek to do the Father's will in the Earth. Pray that they would walk as Messiah walked.

Amen and Amen!

Biography

Batya Wootten and her husband, Angus, were early pioneers in the Messianic movement. Decades ago they began publishing the first Messianic Materials Catalogue, created to serve a fledgling new interest in Israel and the Jewish people.

Batya read countless books about these subjects so she could write informed descriptions of them for the catalogue, and so discovered the great diversity of opinions about Israel's role in the world and about Israel's identity.

Hungering to truly know the truth of the matter, she began to cry out in desperation to her Heavenly Father, asking Him to show her *His* truth. As promised, He answered: "Call to Me and I will answer you, and I will tell you great and mighty things, which you do not know" (Jeremiah 33:3). The Holy One began to open up the Scriptures to her, and His answers led to the writing of many books about Israel and its full restoration.

Batya's challenging books represent decades of study, discussion, and prayer on the crucial issues of identifying Israel, celebrating her feasts, honoring Torah, and the role of women, as well as the importance of the Holy Spirit, the *Ruach haKodesh*. Many readers have given testimony about having been transformed by her informative writings. Lives continue to be changed as they see the truth about Judah and Ephraim and their restoration. It is a truth that is helping to restore a brotherhood broken apart long ago. Her emphasis on the need to show mercy and grace to both houses is helping to heal the wounds that began when Israel was divided into two Kingdoms.

Her book, *Israel's Feasts and Their Fullness: Expanded Edition,* also represents many years of meticulous research, study, and prayerful writing. It is helping Believers to be liberated into glorious celebrations of the feasts. Several people have said of it,

"This is the best book about the feasts that I have ever read." Her book, *Mama's Torah: The Role of Women,* has likewise received high acclaim from both men and women. She also offers a jointly authored "companion" work: *Israel—Empowered by The Spirit,* by Wallace E. Smith and Batya Wootten, plus this overview of her many works about Israel: *Who is Israel? Israel Revealed--A Primer.*

Batya is married to her best friend, Col. Angus Wootten (USA Ret.), author of the visionary books, *Restoring Israel's Kingdom* and *Take Two Tablets Daily.* Together they have ten children who have blessed them with many beloved offspring.

Working as a team, Angus and Batya moved forward from the early days of the *House of David Catalogue* and began publishing a Newsletter, the *House of David Herald.* They also founded the informative Messianic Israel web site: *messianicisrael.com.* This led to the birth of the Messianic Israel Alliance— a rapidly growing and loosely affiliated Alliance of fellowships that agree with "The Hope of Messianic Israel," which is a broad statement of faith.

Together Angus and Batya publish books that serve the growing army of Believers who are discovering the truth about their Hebraic heritage. They work to help raise up new leaders and to draw out their particular giftings. For this assignment they have been uniquely prepared by the God of Abraham, Isaac, and Jacob. We know you will be blessed as you read their works.

Batya posts the following notice in all of her books:

The Word tells us to " let the one who is taught share all good things with him who teaches" (Gal 6:6). If through this book a good thing has been accomplished in your life, please write and share your good news with me.

Batya Wootten, PO Box 700217, Saint Cloud, FL 34770
e-mail addresses: batya@mim.net
batya@keyofdavidpublishing.com

Key of David Publications

Our Most Popular Books

Redeemed Israel—Reunited and Restored by Batya Wootten. Batya's inspiring books are causing a stir, even sparking a reformation. She clearly explains the truth about both houses of Israel (Isa 8:14) and has helped many thousands to discover their Hebraic heritage. Read and understand Israel and the Church, YHVH's master plan for all Israel, Torah's place in our lives, and our latter-day call. This book details our coming restoration. Includes maps, lists, charts, helpful graphics. Paper, 256 pages. $14.95. ISBN 1-886987-21-0 Audio, 6 CDs. $24.95. ISBN 978-1-886987-34-0

Who is Israel? Redeemed Israel—A Primer An overview of Batya's classic works. Quickly outlines the essence of the phenomenal truth about Ephraim and Judah. Offers maps, charts, lists, clarifies Israel and the Church. Helps non-Jewish Believers see their role in the last days. An encouraging book and invaluable tool. Paper, 96 pages, $4.95. ISBN 978-1-886987-39-5. Multiple copies: 3 - $12, 5 - $18, 10 - $30, 25 - $60, 50 - $110, 100 - $200 Audio, 3 CDs, $14.95 ISBN 978-1-886987-30-2

Israel's Feasts and their Fullness: Expanded Edition by Batya Wootten. An informative, liberating classic! Written especially for those who see both houses of Israel. Well research-ed, insightful, enjoyable. Encourages free-dom in Messiah, yet shows reverence for

Scripture and due respect for Judaism's honorable traditions. This work addresses the Shabbat, the seven Feasts, it includes simple "Instruction Guides" for Sabbath, Havdalah, Passover, plus it offers charts, tables, and graphics. Batya's style has endeared her to many thousands of readers. She now invites us to truly celebrate in the presence of the Almighty! Paper, 384 pages, $16.95   ISBN 978-1-886987-29-7

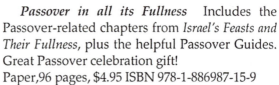

Passover in all its Fullness Includes the Passover-related chapters from *Israel's Feasts and Their Fullness*, plus the helpful Passover Guides. Great Passover celebration gift!
Paper,96 pages, $4.95 ISBN 978-1-886987-15-9

Come! Let Us Rehearse the Four Passovers DVD! Dance filled two-hour drama narrated by Angus and Batya Wootten. Presents Passover based on Scripture. Depicts four Passover types: Family, Congregational, Personal, and Kingdom. See Passover dramatized! Hear the related verses! Exciting, enlightening, encouraging. This two hour DVD will inspire you to celebrate Messiah's Passover like never before! $10.00

Restoring Israel's Kingdom by Angus Wootten. The disciples' last question to Messiah was *when* would He restore Israel's kingdom (Acts 1:6). He told us to pray, *"Your kingdom come. Your will be done, on Earth as it is in heaven."* He proclaimed "the gospel of the kingdom" and said it must be "preached in the whole world…then the end will come" (Mat 6:10; 24:14). Have we lost sight of the vision that once burned in the hearts of His disciples? Do we understand His Gospel? Do we have the same goal He had? This inspiring book will help you keep your eye on His goal. Paper, 304 pages, $14.95 ISBN 1-886987-04-1

Mama's Torah: The Role of Women (NEW! Expanded Edition) by Batya Wootten. This insightful book is getting rave reviews from both men and women. It defines "helpmeet," delightfully depicts the roles of husband and wife, shows how women in Scripture were used, addresses difficult verses, and it unveils the Father's particular call to women for this hour, especially in regard to the spirit of Torah.
Paper, 160 pages, $9.95 ISBN 987- 1-886987-20-3
Audio, 3 CDs $14.95, ISBN 978-1-886987-31-9
Video DVD teaching $10

www.keyofdavidpublishing.com

The Voice... Hearing the Almighty by Batya Wootten. Israel's patriarchs all heard the voice of the Holy One and we should too. Man tends to fear hearing the Almighty. This book explains why. Yah said, *"In the latter days you will return to YHVH your God and listen to His voice"* (Deu 4:30). Difficult times are at our door. We need to learn to hear His voice—right now—today!
Paper, 160 pages, $9.95 ISBN 1-886987-27-0
Audio, 4 CD's, $17.95, ISBN 978-1-886987-36-4

Israel—Empowered by The Spirit by Wallace E. Smith and Batya Ruth Wootten. If you know about your Hebraic roots, yet long for a true move of the Holy Spirit, this book is for you! Finally, a book about the Ruach haKodesh for Messianics! It explains why we especially need the Holy Spirit, addresses counterfeit moves, prayer languages, prophecy, singing in the Spirit, words of wisdom and knowledge, gifts of healing, working of miracles, discerning of spirits, and deliverance. Offers a fascinating explanation of the Urim and Thummim of the High Priest and encourages us to release the Spirit within! An important handbook! Paper, 256 pages, $14.95. ISBN 978-1-886987-28-9
Audio, 5 CDs, $21.95. ISBN 978-1-886987-32-6

In Search of Israel by Batya Ruth Wootten. Who Is Israel? Your answer determines your interpretation of Scripture. This book defines the two houses of Israel - Ephraim and Judah. This is Batya's first book published in 1988.
Paper, 148 Pages, $9.95, ISBN 0-914903-56-X
Audio, 3 CDs, $14.95, ISBN 978-1-886987-35-7

¿Quien Es Israel? by Batya Wootten, translated by Natalie Pavlik. The truth about both the houses of Israel that is inspiring Believers everywhere. Spanish version of the classic *Who Is Israel? And Why You Need To Know*. Paper, 304 pages. $14.95. ISBN 1-886987-08-1

Take Two Tablets Daily: The 10 Command-ments and 613 Laws by Angus Wootten. Lists the 613 Mosaic laws (divided into Mandatory Commandments and Prohibitions) and gives the source Scripture(s). YHVH's Word is like medicine and nothing better symbolizes His Word than the two "tablets" on which He wrote His Covenant. Taken daily, these "Two Tablets" will give us life more abundantly. This easy reference book should be in every library. Paper, 96 pages, $4.95   ISBN 1-886987-06-8

Return to the Land: An Ephraimite's Journey Home by Ephraim Frank. Ephraim could not explain what he felt burning in his soul. He only knew that he was being drawn, wooed by His God and had gone on a tour that had forever changed his life... From the farm lands of America to the Holy Land of Israel this compelling auto-biography tells of a "stranger" who felt divinely drawn to the Promised Land and the God of Abraham, Isaac, and Jacob. It tells of the birthing of a new move of the Holy One, gently reveals what He is doing in the Earth today, and tells of the blessed redemption of *all* Israel. Paper, 240 pages, $12.95   ISBN 1-886987-18-1

For a full listing of all books from Key of David Publishing
Visit: www.keyofdavidpublishing.com
Email: admin@keyofdavidpublishing.com
Phone: 407.344.7700. Write: PO Box 700217, Saint Cloud, 34770
You can listen to the first several chapters of Audio Books,
and download them from Paper Books at the website.
Quantity Discounts Available

Books also are available at:
Messianic Israel Alliance Marketplace
www.messianicisrael.com Phone: 800.829.8777
Write: PO Box 3263, Lebanon, TN 37088

Coming Soon!
Raptured Onto the Back of a Horse by Batya Wootten